IS GOD ON AMERICA'S SIDE?

MICHAEL J. SUTTON

ISBN: 978-0-6455671-1-3

Published by Hidden Road Publishing

Also available:

Freedom from Fascism, A Christian Response to Mass Formation Psychosis

DEDICATION

To those many Americans who love Jesus and follow him, who open their Bibles and seek to deepen their knowledge and love, who know the difference between faith and flag, and who resist those who try to turn their personal faith in God into a political weapon of hate, distrust, and division, this book is for you.

CONTENTS

ACKNOWLEDGMENTS

There are too many people I need to thank without whom this book would not have been possible. This includes the thousands of pastors, ministers, bishops, and priests in America, who stand up every Sunday and lie to their congregations about God, America, and the future. We all need to make a choice in life, and these men and women have chosen money, power, and reputation over truth and faithfulness to God's word, the Bible. On the Last Day, when we all need to give an account of our life before God, you guys have made God's job a lot easier. This book is for you.

1   FAITH AND FLAG

Is God on America's side? Does God bless America? Do nations have a divine destiny? Is America exceptional? Is America a Christian nation? Many believe the answer to all these questions is a resounding *'yes.'* Many people believe that America is the *'light on the hill,'* the *'great experiment,'* the template for freedom and liberty. These slogans and the assumptions behind them are deeply spiritual, for many people believe that God has ordained America in some intangible, special, exclusive way. Many sincerely believe that since America is blessed by God, it exists by divine right, and therefore, God wishes us to fear America because God walks with Americans and blesses their nation.

From the outset let me be completely honest with you. A nation is like anything in life. How you feel about your nation is entirely up to you. You can love it, or you can loathe it, you can be devoted to it, or dismissive of it, you can support it, or you can spurn it. You are free to do what you like in this respect. I do not judge America, nor could I ever, only God can judge anyone or anything. But I will say this, and I hope you are reading very carefully so you will not misunderstand me: faith and flag are not the same, they never have been and never will be. Those who confuse faith and flag are either those who simply do not know the God whom they claim to follow, or they are fake followers of God. It is as simple as that. I know this with absolute certainty because it is what the Bible says with clarity

1

and precision. Those who seek to justify the marriage between faith and flag through the scriptures are pernicious, deceitful frauds, for it is impossible to read the Bible and reach the conclusion that God is on anyone's side.

This book is about America, it is about fear, and fear of power, which is one of the most powerful fears in our world today. It is also about identity and loyalty, for if we are members of a nation, these questions are intimately connected with nations and nationalism. This book is also about what some call quite erroneously *'Christian Nationalism.'* I take issue with this label as there is absolutely nothing wrong with flag-waving, loving your country, or being a Christian. I know there are many Christians in America, on all sides of the political landscape who follow Christ and who love their country, but they would not call themselves *'Christian nationalists.'* Why don't we call Christian Nationalists out for who they really are? Christians who mix faith and flag in any form, are Christian Fascists. This more recent far-right movement is just an offshoot of a much older, established philosophy that replaces Christ with the church, faith with religion, and the Spirit with political power.

I wrote this book based on a series of blogs and podcasts as part of our Freedom from Fear series at *Freedom Matters Today* in 2022. The context is important. These podcasts were broadcast during the last gasps of the politically crafted Covid Hysteria period of 2019-2022, the beginning of the next stage in the civil war in Ukraine, and the post-Trump American Culture War.

Political identity might seem a strange place to begin a Biblical discussion on the nature of fear, but it is entirely appropriate. Our world is a world shaped by and obsessed with political power and America is now, though not forever, one of the chief centers of power in the world. What Joe Biden says or struggles to say these days, and what America believes and does, is at the heart of global political thought and policy around the world. American power is inescapable, though it is not the only power, nor is it the only nation that has claimed divine right. Spain, Portugal, and Britain are among other nations that at some time believed that God had ordained them to rule the world.

Should we fear nations? Is the fear of America warranted? If it is the case that God is on America's side, then obviously we must fear America because if we do not, we will be fighting against God. But if America is not blessed by God, we are free to do as we choose. This means we are truly free.

2   DOES GOD BLESS AMERICA?

Are you scared?

We live in an age of anxiety. We live in a world of fear. Many of these fears are manufactured. In other words, they are not real, or they are based on a collection of facts bundled together for the purpose of manipulation. They have been crafted, created, sustained, and imprinted on our hearts, minds, and souls by others with power over us. If it is not the government, it is religion, if it is not religion, it is the mob or cultural pressure, if it is not the mob, it is the media. Are you scared? It is hard not to be.

These cultures of fear, these factories of fear, these manufactured anxieties, have one goal: to keep us oppressed. This oppression is achieved by keeping us in a state of perpetual fear and despair. Our minds, hearts, and souls are clay in their hands. We are manipulated, deluded, lied to, deceived, and indoctrinated. This oppression is the goal of people of power in every generation. There is nothing new about the manufacturing of fear and despair.

What is different these days seems to be the deliberate creation of crises for the purpose of social control, especially in nations that boast of being robust democracies. These crises come in succession, neatly, almost too neatly. They are all different, but they are all the same. As one crisis ends, another appears as if out of magic, and then we are forced to think about the new crisis with every fiber of our being. We are told what to think, whom to blame, what to think about, what questions to ask, and God help anyone who challenges, questions, or protests any of it.

The staple of democracies used to be bread and circuses, TV and media, sport and leisure, opulence and materialism, jealousy and contentment. The West was shaken to its foundations by the fall of the Soviet Union in the late 1980s. This earthquake continues to reverberate around the world, even today. The West, once triumphant, teeters on collapse. It certainly has been in decline since the early 1970s due in part to oil shocks, stagflation, and the end of the fixed exchange rate. It was not that the Soviet Union fell, but it fell first. The West is falling because eventually, everything does.

The history of the last five centuries has seen the rise and fall of a dozen empires, and there is no reason to expect that America will not fall into ruin, decay, and disaster. Many people in power in America do not believe history applies to them or their nation. The current triumphalism is seen in expressions such as *'this is the greatest nation in the history of the world,'* or the mantra *'Make America Great Again.'* This is just rhetoric. Historical patterns do not bode well for the future of America. Smart nations try to keep quiet, and strong nations don't need to speak at all. Is it a coincidence that this excitement over restoring American greatness comes at this point in history?

Since 9/11, the West has been under attack from enemies real and imagined. The greatest enemy of the West is truth, the truth about itself, about its lies and inherent deceit, about its greatest fear which is history, for, in history, the West knows that it has a time limit, a ticking clock if you will, an hourglass that continues to drain life and hope from a small group of nations who have denied both to most of the world for the last two centuries.

It is in this world of decline that people in power manufacture anxiety, fear, and despair. These are the pills for our age, the diet for our population, and the nutrition for our people. It is a diet of fear. Chances are, most of the anxieties and fears of today are manufactured by people in power for our oppression. Most of the psychological problems, mental anxieties, and social difficulties are products of the mess the West has created. In particular, the spirit since 9/11 has been to conjure fear, stir up anxiety, and promote despair. This atmosphere is indicative of national decline.

The West tells us that our current enemies are Russia and China. Before long, it will be India and any other nation that threatens the economic power of a tiny group of political and economic elites in the upper strata of society. Unless they have a plan to exterminate 3 to 4 billion people, we must find a way to live with people even with those with whom we disagree. The failure to realize this in the last twenty years is the reason I do not believe the West has much of a future. The ruling class in America, England, France, and Germany will not tolerate a world of shared prosperity. Sadly, the future is a shared world or a dead world, a world of many voices or no voice.

There is also the possibility of the rise of another Babylon, a great nation that seeks to control everything and everyone. I hope not. I sincerely hope that no nation seeks that position, that role, for the Bible teaches that Babylon will be destroyed. All nations that have sought world domination go the same way. You can visit what is left of them in museums these days. They all thought the same way some of our leaders do today.

Strong nations do not bother with such strategies of manufactured fear. We live at a time when democracy is falling after a century of being the façade of English and American power. As this power wanes declines, and shifts, nations are becoming more paranoid about social control. Thus, manufactured anxiety is the tool of people in power to control the masses because they fear the very thing they pretend democracy is about – freedom.

It is time to revisit fear and despair, not the demons and phantoms produced by the state or the media, or the military, but real fears. Many people in society fight for freedom, many work in dark places, many work alone, and many work under pressure and persecution. Many do not share the same political philosophy, some are Marxists, some Libertarians, some social democrats, and some liberals, but these countervailing forces stand for freedom. I stand with them, for even though we may differ on many points, those who stand for freedom these days stand for truth.

But at *Freedom Matters Today*, we have a unique approach. We consider freedom from a Christian perspective and approach the issue with an open Bible. If you have read my first book, you know where I stand. If you a Christian Nationalist or Christian Fascist you probably burnt my book, or cast it away in horror, for I do not stand with you. We promote Christianity not religion, we follow Jesus, not the church, we promote the kingdom of God, not the kingdom of earth. We do not take sides. We are non-sectarian and apolitical.

This book is a different kind of book, and our starting point is different. Our starting point is the Bible. We ignore church traditions. We follow the text of the scriptures and dismiss the politics of the church. This makes enemies and we have made a few. I hear that *'Christian Nationalism'* is popular today. Why they call it *'nationalism'* I don't know. There is nothing wrong with loving your nation, flying your flag, singing your anthem, and even wearing your flag as an item of clothing. I am an Australian and I love my country. I was born here, and it is the nation of my birth. I am also a Christian, which means I follow Jesus. I am not, however, a Christian Nationalist, nor ever will be. There is no such thing. One cannot be a Christian and a Christian Nationalist. Faith and flag are not the same, never have been, and never will be.

Christian Nationalism is a form of Christian Fascism, and at *Freedom Matters Today*, we stand against fascism. We promote freedom from fascism and tyranny and fascism is a form of tyranny, even fascism in the name of God. Now is the time to make a fortune lying about God and the Bible, and lying about church and state, and lying about God and America. Politicians in America are gearing up for the 2024 Presidential election, and many Christians want a Christian President, with Christian values, and a return to a Christian nation. I stand against you. The truth always matters more than politics and money, and I will stand for the truth every time because I believe in God and one day I will stand before him and give an account of my life.

What is truth? Truth has a name, and his name is Jesus Christ. Beyond knowing God and being known by God, Christian politics does not exist in the kingdom of God. I make no apology for offending the church or Christians. Fascism is evil, a disease of faith, and an instrument of human power and ambition. History is against you, dear fascists. Do you hear the voices of the millions slaughtered by the church, their blood crying out for justice, their cries reaching to the heavens? Your Christian Nationalism is just another form of evil dressed up in the clothes of religion. Jesus said: *'my kingdom is not of this world'* (John 18: 36), and Paul says, *'flesh and blood cannot inherit the kingdom of God'* (1 Corinthians 15: 50). But the Christian Nationalist will not let the Word of God get in the way of their political ambitions.

In our first book, titled *'Freedom from Fascism: A Christian Response to Mass Formation Psychosis,'* we exposed the evil of Christian Fascism, which is the truth about institutional religion in the Western world. To be sure, the regimes of Communism, Fascism, and Democracy in the last two centuries have, from time to time, lurched into terrible darkness, but this is nothing compared to the hell, the horror, and the misery of a world run by the Christian church. For centuries, the religious elites caused unspeakable suffering in the world, subjecting hundreds of millions to persecution, torture, deprivation, starvation, and misery.

Christian Fascism is not Christianity, and these fascists are not Christians. Christianity is about Jesus, his identity, his life, his accomplishments, and our response to him, not about religion, rituals, and rules. Faith leads to God, but religion leads to the church. The great Christian struggle has not been against the state but against the church, for the church is not the defender of the faith, Christ is, as he stands for and defends his people. Given the corruption, nepotism, and criminality of the Western Church, the state needs to step in and reform the Christian Church for the sake of Christianity and the nation. Not surprisingly, fascists in the church denounce me as a heretic. In previous eras, I would have been executed by the church-state for daring to step beyond the acceptable religious boundary which is *'sit down, shut up, and do as you are told.'*

Freedom from Fascism was anchored in a key verse from the New Testament. This verse was one of the sayings of Jesus, which was taken from John's Gospel, chapter 14, and verse 6: *'I am the way, and the truth and the life, no one comes to the Father but through me.'* Christian Fascists don't care about how Christ changes our hearts, they are interested in forcing change in the world. In *Freedom from Fascism,* we discovered that Christian churches have mistranslated the word *'assembly'* which means a gathering of people and replaced it with the word *'church'* which means a building or a place. It did this to ensure power and control, and that you listened to them and not the Holy Spirit.

Fascism takes the authority of choice away from us and gives it to someone else to decide in our place what we ought to believe in. God, on the other hand, wants us to decide for ourselves, and he gives us a mind, a heart, and a will to enable us to do just that. If

God is anything, he is patient, he is not in a rush, he tolerates all our questions, doubts, and uncertainties, and wants us to know him. Knowing God is the heart of Christianity: simply to know God and be known by him.

Jesus also came to set us free from fear, which is perhaps more dangerous than fascism because at least with fascism, it can be identified and understood. At the same time, however, the institutional church is an active obstacle in navigating the spiritual landscape of fear. Our contemporary understanding of fear is mistranslated and misapplied by Christian Fascists for the same reason they tampered with the word *'church'* – they want to present a twisted, sick, and dark image of God, a God who is forever angry, forever elusive, and forever unattainable. This is not the God of the Bible.

The God of the Bible has come to calm fear, to replace despair with hope, and anxiety with peace. This may not be the Christianity you have heard of before. Most people think that we can only stand before God with closed eyes and clenched fists anticipating disapproval and punishment. That is how Christian Fascism expects you to stand before them in their churches. But not God. He has come to bring hope, for he is our hope.

Is America Exceptional?

When I was at university, the internet was still in its infancy, cable TV was something they had in America, we had a few free-to-air TV channels, many media companies, and diverse ownership of print media. In those days, few people ever gave national politics much consideration except around election time or if you worked in vulnerable sectors such as old-fashioned manufacturing or agricultural industries. In the 1980s, this began to change because of higher interest rates for mortgages, and this was reflected in the appearance of finance segments on the evening news. Politics became more important. Even so, what happened in America didn't affect people unless they were Americans or had an interest in international relations.

9/11 changed all of this. I was abroad at the time and living in the beautiful city of Sendai, in northern Japan. I was astounded at how this happened, but I was not stupid, of course, I knew why – it was clear that American foreign policies in the Middle East were partly to blame. America spent most of the post-war era interfering in or seeking to secure access to oil and other resources in the Middle East. Many people love America, but many also hate America. I was surprised that a terrorist attack had not happened in America sooner. I guess they were stopped.

A good American friend at the time asked me why 9/11 happened, and I could not give him an answer. As a Christian, I do not know the mind of God. I cannot possibly know why these things happen, but I gave him a book on American foreign policy in the Middle East. I cannot remember which one. He read it and told me a few weeks later that he could understand how his country interfered in the lives of other nations and he could see the economic and strategic roots behind the terrorist attack. The guy went to work for the American government. God bless him wherever he is. The principle I was talking about is simple: it is cause and effect. It is a basic principle of international relations and history. The actions of nations usually have reasons behind them. These reasons are often clear and strategic, or they are stupid. All nations behave in the same way.

When you go to university you might study nations and you will come across several points of view. The first is liberalism which is an idealist view and places its emphasis on cooperation between nations, and the role and influence of individuals. The second is realism, which is a practical view that places its emphasis on the nation-state and has the view that nations compete against each other. The third view is Marxism, which places its emphasis on class, and the idea of class struggle between the worker and the capitalist. These three views are the main schools of thought in the academy. All three views are the mechanical way of understanding how nations work. They are all the same in the sense they are all highly respected.

After 9/11, I became aware of another view, one coming from America. It is an idea. The ancients had a name for it too. It was idolatry. Most nations in the past understood idol worship. They had many idols. Greece had them. Rome had them, many ancient nations had them. These idols were images of gods, demons, monsters, and other beings, supernatural or natural to whom people could present their requests and prayers. Rome sometimes deified her emperors for example. Cities often had gods protecting them or idols crafted to sit in homes or places of worship. Idols were common across the ancient world.

The idea I saw coming out of America was that of *'exceptionalism,'* the belief that America is special, that it is blessed by God, that it is a *'light on the hill'* for all nations, that God has touched it and blessed it, that it is exceptional and beyond the rules of other nations, beyond the ancient rules of life, and beyond the judgment of God and justice. Many American Christians are Christian Fascists of one stripe or another and if you ask them, they will subscribe to the idea, that America is God's nation. America, they say, has a purpose in God's plan for the world, that America is the great experiment for freedom and democracy, and that America is the home of all that is good, virtuous, and true. We see this view expressed in their Culture War.

Now, there is nothing wrong with patriotism and loving your nation. All people come from a nation of some description, excluding the millions of stateless people who have no home. Exceptionalism is different because it preaches the idea that one nation has a special destiny that gives it the right to rise above others. The problem with exceptionalism is that it is not true. America is just another nation. It operates in the same way as other nations, it is not special, it is not the light on the hill and God is not with her. The problem is not America of course, but the American church which has been peddling this nonsense for generations. They mix faith, and flag to such a degree that where one ends and the other begins is impossible to discern. This is American Christian Fascism. This is the dominant thread of American Christianity. Is America exceptional? Yes, but for all the wrong reasons.

It is the reason why most non-Christian Americans cannot stand the church and will never go. In addition, it is the reason for most of America's social problems and it is the reason why America continues to go to war abroad, it is driven by the religious fanaticism of millions of people who have never opened their Bible and yet believe that the God of the Bible supports their nation in every single action, simply because they are Americans. They cannot tell the difference between God and America, between Jesus and the USA, and between the Bible and the US Constitution. Is America exceptional? Yes, in some ways. Only Americans could destroy Christian witness so decisively and comprehensively in such a short period of time.

At this point, you might say, well who cares? That is America. Well, this idolatry of exceptionalism is being exported around the world and many Christians around the world are falling for it, this hideous, twisted *'Christian nationalism'* or American-led Christian Fascism. This took off during the years following 9/11. The West in general began to follow America more closely and get caught up in American politics. Soon, America became the center of our politics, our society, our way of thinking, and our culture. When Trump was elected in 2016, the madness began. I am not talking about Trump. We all have an opinion of him. I don't care what yours is. The madness was the obsession with Trump, everything he said, everything he did, and everything he did not do.

The madness continued in 2020 and now is getting worse. Nations are being sucked into the vortex, into the hurricane that is America, and its idolatry of exceptionalism. Misplaced fears and crafted anxieties. That is America's gift to the West. The product of false exceptionalism, the failure to decline gracefully and powerfully, with respect. This is chaos, it is disorder, it is division, it is madness.

It is not Black Lives Matter, it is only black Americans that matter, it is not the end of racial problems, it is the end of America's racial problems, it is not *'world peace,'* but peace in America, it is not economic stability in the world, but economic stability in America, it is not global human rights, but American human rights. Therefore, it is not freedom that matters but only America that matters. Many Americans are obsessed with themselves and their nation. They believe themselves to be beyond criticism and beyond even God himself.

At the heart of all of this is fear: fear of Covid, fear of the war in Ukraine and possible nuclear war, fear of war with Russia, and war with China, fear of economic decline, fear of rising interest rates, fear of racism and sexism and fear of climate change, and fear of censorship, misinformation, and fake news. All of this comes from America. It is also indicative of American decline, or America's failure to handle or manage strategic realignment. All of these are the crafted crises and anxieties of the state.

During the Ukraine Civil War, many Christian speakers and pastors have reached back into the past and pulled out all the Cold War rhetoric they used against Russia. For many American Christians, America's enemies are God's enemies. They falsely claim that Russia is the Gog and Magog of the Hebrew Bible, twisting the prophecies of Ezekiel and arguing that this is the End Times. It is remarkable that the only enemies in the Bible just happen to be all of America's enemies or rivals. None of these charlatans ever see America as anything other than the vessel for God's power. Vanity, vanity, all is vanity and chasing after the wind. But it sounds good, and they rake in the money from the naïve and fearful Christians who have taken their eyes off Christ and placed them on these frauds and liars.

This is not leadership; it is insanity, and it is the result of idolatry. It is the product of exceptionalism. This is not a nation walking with God. It is a nation walking alone. What does the Bible say about America? That is a very good question, and it is what this book is all about.

Did Jesus ever turn anyone away?

What we know today is a world of fears and these fears shape our lives, but should they? Should we give them the attention we do? Do we need to? Many of these fears stem from America and the belief that it is exceptional. If this is true, then many of these fears deserve our attention. If it is false, and America is not exceptional, then we can dismiss them all as fake news. In other words, the fear is not the fear of America, after all, there is always a nation like America, and there are many nations like America in the world. The fear is that there is some special relationship between America and God. Many people in the world believe that there is, that God is on America's side, that God is blessing America, and that America lives under the protection of God.

The problem is that Christianity does not begin with the Western Church, it does not begin with America, and does not rest upon American ideas about God. The New Testament makes a clear distinction between the people of Israel and the rest of humanity. This is offensive to many Western Christians who believe that the church is Western and that it began with St Peter and Rome or the Orthodox Church, or the Protestant Church. They have spent two thousand years purging the Bible of Jewish content, origins, and doctrine, and have created incoherent monstrosities such as the Mass and the Church. There is nothing more Anti-Semitic in the church than the Mass. This desire to cleanse the church of Jews led to the Holocaust and continues to place Jewish people in a precarious position around the world.

Part of this confusion is a word that I have never really understood – the word *'Gentile.'* It is not a Greek word, and it is not found in the New Testament, but it is a word that defines and encapsulates much about our understanding of who we are in relation to God and God's chosen people, the Jews. The second part of this confusion has to do with the state of Israel in today's Palestine, and the American response to Israel.

Why isn't the word translated properly? The word translated as *'Gentiles'* occurs many times in the New Testament. I do not know why we use the word. The original Greek word is not surprising. As soon as you hear it spoken in Greek, you know what it means, and it all becomes clear. That word is *ethnos*. You guessed it, this is where we get our word *ethnicity*, or *ethnic*. We are all members of an ethnic group. Why don't English translators sometimes translate the word properly? The word 'Gentile' is redundant and obsolete.

The word ethnos in Greek is sometimes translated as *'the nations,'* or the *'nation.'* These nations are ethnically distinct from the other category mentioned in the New Testament, the Jews. Being Jewish was not simply a religious affiliation or cultural one, but an ethnic and national affiliation. The nation of Israel, the Jewish people, existed since Abraham and continued well beyond the days of Jesus. Israel never ceased to be a nation. Why does the New Testament make the distinction between *'the nations,'* and Israel? Why is Israel singled out for attention? This is a good question, and many have asked it. Christians have their answers, and few are satisfactory. Entire books have been written on the subject, but I would rather point you to a short text in one of the Gospels that highlights the problem for us.

Sadly, and for me as well, the story is deeply offensive. It is worse than what Paul writes in Romans about Israel (Romans 9), and it is deeply humbling for a man who is not Jewish as far as I know. The

Gospel writers were honest people. If they had any intention of gaining as much support as they could, they would have omitted this story. They did not, and we have, in this short episode, a story where Jesus turned a person away because she was not Jewish.

There is an encounter between Jesus and a woman from *'the nations'* recorded in the Gospels of Matthew (Chapter 15) and Mark (Chapter 7). It is essentially the same story, but it is not a pleasant one and has offended many over the years. They are offended because they are brought up to believe in their church that Jesus came for English-speaking people, for Americans, and that Jesus is America's God or the God of English-speaking civilization.

In their eyes, God can only be worshipped with the right intonation of voice, the right tone, and the right accent. Nothing else will do. The church must be built in a certain style, with certain architectural features and aspects, and seating arrangements. Since the nineteenth century, England, Australia, America, Germany, and other Western nations have sent missionaries around the world to convince *'the nations'* not only that Jesus is Lord, but that Jesus wants us all to be Western and civilized, with the right values, culture, and aspirations. These fascists sit back and say things like *'well, we brought them civilization,'* or *'we saved them from their dark ways,'* or *'their culture was wretched and sinful.'* Missionaries do not bring the Bible, but the *'Bible+'* which is the Bible plus values, plus attitudes and structures, insisting that everyone adopt Western ways, worship in Western styles, and speak English.

I will look at Matthew 15: 21-28. Matthew writes:

'Leaving that place, Jesus withdrew to the region of Tyre and Sidon. A Canaanite woman from that vicinity came to him, crying out, "Lord, Son of David, have mercy on me! My daughter is demon-possessed and suffering terribly." Jesus did not answer a word. So, his disciples came to him and urged him, "Send her away, for she keeps crying out after us." He answered, "I was sent only to the lost sheep of Israel." The woman came and knelt before him. "Lord, help me!" she said. He replied, "It is not right to take the children's bread and toss it to the dogs." "Yes, it is, Lord," she said. "Even the dogs eat the crumbs that fall from their master's table." Then Jesus said to her, "Woman, you have great faith! Your request is granted." And her daughter was healed at that moment.'

There are a few things to notice about this passage. It presents an uncomfortable image of Jesus. It suggests that he might be racist. Despite the pleas of the woman, *'Jesus did not answer a word.'* How could you? How could you ignore the pleas of the suffering? Jesus expresses no interest in the woman or her complaint. Even after the complaints of his disciples, all Jesus says is *'I was sent only to the lost sheep of Israel.'*

This itself is instructive, for they are the words of Jesus and we do well to dwell upon them. They are humbling words. Jesus is not lying, for if we believe in the divinity of Christ as many Christians claim to, then he was speaking the truth and how deeply humbling this is to hear. He did not come for *'the nations,'* but for the *'lost sheep of Israel.'* America was not his primary concern during his earthly mission in Palestine. He was not thinking of England, nor *'did those feet in ancient time, walk upon England's mountains green,'* as William Blake mused.

Jesus is in Tyre and Sidon, which was outside of Palestine or Israel during his time, in the north, above Galilee. Previously in Matthew's account, Jesus had an unpleasant encounter with some members of the sect of the Pharisees (Matthew 15: 1-20). The Pharisees were an important political and religious party in the decades before the fall of Jerusalem in AD 70. Paul had been a member, and while there were significant differences, the theology of Christ and the Pharisees overlapped. Nonetheless, Jesus and the Pharisees often clashed and argued over the nature of the kingdom of God, and after this confrontation, he departs and ends up in Tyre and Sidon. Once there, he is confronted with the same problems he encountered in Israel: people in oppression seeking his help.

From our perspective, Jesus is very rude to the woman. He turns her away. He expresses no interest. He is not here for her. He tells her that he came for the *'lost sheep of Israel,'* in other words, I did not come for the people of Tyre or Sidon but for the Jews. It is a phrase with prophetic tones and echoes some of the rhetoric used by the prophets of ancient times. He reminds his audience, his disciples, followers, onlookers, and supplicants, that he is here for Israel. He is their Messiah. Some American pastors claim that Jesus never identified as being the Messiah. Are they illiterate? Perhaps. The entire New Testament is a clear and decisive proclamation of the case for Jesus being the Messiah of God, the long-awaited anointed one of God, spoken of in Isaiah, Ezekiel, and the other prophetic writings.

But what Jesus says to the woman is a remarkable statement. It is astounding. Jesus continues to astound us. If you read the Bible and are no longer astounded, no longer challenged, no longer humbled, and no longer inspired, then you are asleep. One can follow Jesus for one's entire life and on the day of one's death be astounded once more by the words, the ideas, the life, and the identity of Jesus of Nazareth. Let me repeat what Jesus said in today's language so there is no ambiguity: *'I did not come for the Americans, I am not here for America, or England, or the West, but for Israel.'*

Thank God that Jesus was speaking with this woman for her response is even more remarkable. She is not a good American. I am sorry. She isn't. There is no argument, no assertion of her Constitutional rights, no presumption, no pontificating, no defense of individualism, not even an appeal to Caesar. Her response indicates that she accepts the words of Jesus, she accepts her place in his understanding of the world no matter how offensive it is, no matter how hurtful those words are. Her response is one of deep humility and self-abasement. Could you respond in the way she does?

History has ignored her, like history ignores most women in the New Testament, except for the mad hagiography around Mary, the mother of Jesus, and the fiction about Magdalene. Without the assistance of women, Jesus would not have been able to financially sustain his ministry. It was not men who supplied his financial needs (Luke 8: 3). The history of the church is written by men, often men who have oppressed women and lied to them about the relationship between Christ and women. The great obscenity in the Australian church is that women are *'equal but different.'* This is not only heresy, but it echoes another vile evil this time in America, that of segregation, and it is probably where the Australian slogan comes from: *'equal but separate.'* Both are Satanic expressions. Both Paul and Peter emphasize in their writings that men and women are co-heirs of Christ (1 Peter 3: 7, Romans 8:17).

The text speaks for itself. The words of Jesus hurt the woman but do not stop her, they are designed to stop her, but she is better than that. She believes Jesus can and will heal her daughter and falls at his feet. She will not give up on her nearest and dearest. Jesus repeats himself and refers to non-Jewish people as dogs. Imagine that. What an insult. *'It is not right to take the children's bread and toss it to the dogs.'* Is this the Jesus you have read about? Is this the Jesus that is presented in your church? According to Jesus Christ, Americans are dogs as are all those who are not Jewish. We are not children of God, we are not born as children of God, and we are outside of Israel. But even this doesn't stop her. This remarkable woman agrees with Jesus. She does not dispute his assertion, and she rebukes him with her answer – *'even the dogs eat the crumbs under the table.'*

The text states that her response surprises Jesus to the point where he confesses that not only does this foreign woman have faith but that her faith is great. Her daughter is healed. I believe Jesus was amazed not only by her position in life, that she was a foreigner, but because she had engaged in a brief debate with Jesus, and prevailed. Not even the Pharisees with all their learning had anything like the ability of this woman. The episode records no pauses, no contemplation; this woman was deeply wise and astute, and she didn't give Jesus any room to move.

She also revealed to us a deeper intent, the heart of Christ to heal all people, regardless of their nation of origin. Even a foreigner who is outside of Israel could have faith in Jesus. This is an example of a woman who is so desperate for healing that she seeks to overturn the mandate of the Messiah. She will not take no for an answer and even if Jesus came not for her, but for the Jews, he would bring healing to her daughter because she would not let go until he healed her. There are echoes of this stream of thought in the life of Jesus in Luke 18, and Matthew 7:9. Even though the Messiah came for Israel, the faith of the woman could not be repudiated if Christ was the Messiah. If he refused her even with her *'great faith,'* then he was not the Messiah of God. God turns no one away, and he will not even refuse the outsiders. Indeed, the mission of Jesus included those outside Israel (Luke 4: 24-7).

This episode brings to my mind the most enigmatic verse of the Gospels, which is often correctly translated, but rarely understood and usually ignored by the church because they don't know what to make of it. It is Matthew 11: 12: *'From the days of John the Baptist until now, the kingdom of heaven has been subjected to violence, and violent people have been raiding it.'* This woman is one such person who will stop at nothing to find her answers from the man from Nazareth. Jesus is not using the term *'violence'* in the way we understand it. It is an unusual Greek word, and most translators use the term *'violence,'* though it could mean being forceful or even assertive. As I understand the context, I would suggest it would mean that people *'will stop at nothing to enter the kingdom of God.'* This woman is one such person. She will not take no for an answer. This assertiveness, this desire for healing, this approach to God, this all-encompassing scope of God's love for all, this is Christianity.

While the church tries to ignore this episode, there are more ambiguities related to the way English-speaking people navigate our relationship with Israel. Another example is Luke 2: 25-32. Luke writes:

'Now there was a man in Jerusalem called Simeon, who was righteous and devout. He was waiting for the consolation of Israel, and the Holy Spirit was on him. It had been revealed to him by the Holy Spirit that he would not die before he had seen the Lord's Messiah. Moved by the Spirit, he went into the temple courts. When the parents brought in the child Jesus to do for him what the custom of the Law required, Simeon took him in his arms and praised God, saying:
"Sovereign Lord, as you have promised,
  you may now dismiss your servant in peace.
For my eyes have seen your salvation,
  which you have prepared in the sight of all nations:
a light for revelation to the Gentiles,
  and the glory of your people Israel."'

This text is commonly used in the Christmas rites, or during nativity plays where a little white ceramic Jesus is cuddled by kids speaking English. The text is confusing because it does not convey the original meaning in some translations, and I am not sure why this meaning is obscured. The phrase *'light for revelation to the Gentiles,'* is not in the original. It reads *'to the nations'* or *'to the ethnos,'* and the word *'Gentile'* is an imported word, not a word arising from the text. The previous verse *'in the sight of all nations'*

(2:31) is also not translated correctly in the New International Version (NIV). Most translations render the verse: *'in the sight of all people,'* or variations of this. It should read something like this: *'...which you have prepared in the sight of all people, a light for revelation to the nations, and the glory of your people Israel.'*

In other words, the arrival of the Messiah is for everyone, and this provides the preface for the introduction of the two groups of nations in the world, the Jewish nation, and the other nations. The benefit of the Messiah comes to both differently. For the nations outside of Israel, it is truly a revelation that the Messiah comes through Israel, and they come to faith through revelation, through this new understanding. By contrast, glory comes to Israel as the people to whom the Messiah would come. It would be a revelation to the nations that were without the promises, the patriarchs, and the prophets (See also Ephesians 2: 11-13). The arrival of Jesus is glory for Israel, those close by, and revelation to the nations, those far away.

This distinction is strengthened in the original. In Greek, the word *'revelation'* in this verse is where we get our word *'apocalypse'* but it generally means an unveiling or an uncovering of something. In this context, the unveiling concerns the truth about the Messiah Jesus. It is a surprise to the nations, especially as they were not prepared to hear or receive the message. The contrast could not be more striking when we consider the phrase *'and glory of your people Israel.'* Unlike the nations, Israel has a special place in God's heart. The arrival of the Messiah conveys to God's people glory. It is often something that describes the character of God rather than people. We tend to associate glory with God, such as the phrase *'we do this for God's glory,'* but here, this *'glory to the people of Israel'* suggests that Israel's reputation and honor in the world are exalted and elevated since the Messiah is one of their number, the Messiah comes from them, he is a man born of a woman born under the Law (Galatians 4:4).

As Westerners, we tend to assume that we are active participants in the gospels. We are not. We are outsiders, foreigners, those who are far away as Paul tells us (Ephesians 2: 13). The ministry of Jesus was primarily among the Jewish people. There were exceptions such as the woman of Samaria (John 4), the Roman Centurion (Matthew 8: 5-13), and the Canaanite woman (Matthew 15: 21-28). These stories function to highlight the severity of the rejection of Jesus by his own people in contrast to the eagerness of these outsiders to embrace Christ. These encounters function in a similar way to the widow of Zarephath in the story of Elijah to condemn Israel, an allusion Jesus mentions in his infamous speech at Nazareth that precipitated the first serious attempt on his life (Luke 4: 18-27).

This was all to change. There was a moment in the life of Jesus when he realises that his Father has all the pieces in place. Again, it is a little glimpse into the thought of Christ. Jesus wrote no texts, and the gospels are all that remains of the authentic life of Jesus, and from time to time, on the edge of the text, or beneath it, we get a little insight into a deeper world, the thinking of Jesus concerning timing, and strategy. We don't know how or why Jesus thought this, and we have no indication as far as I can tell that this was the sign, but in John's account of the life of Jesus, this is the moment.

'Now there were some Greeks among those who went up to worship at the festival. They came to Philip, who was from Bethsaida in Galilee, with a request. "Sir," they said, "we would like to see Jesus." Philip went to tell Andrew; Andrew and Philip in turn told Jesus. Jesus replied, "The hour has come for the Son of Man to be glorified' (John 12: 20-22).

It is only at the end of his public ministry that we Greeks or foreigners make our entrance. They are not there for healing, nor do they bring some questions, nor are they there to debate him. They simply want to *'see him.'* Yet the Greeks never get to speak to Jesus as far as we know. Events begin to spiral, there is the betrayal, the trial, and the execution. It is left to Peter, Paul, and Philip to take the good news to those outside the Jewish nation. We naturally assume as Westerners that Jesus is already there for us, that he is already the Savior of the world. Yet we forget that he came for Israel and that we are those of the nations, the nations of the revelation of God, not the people of the promises of God. Through Christ, other nations come into the kingdom of God that was promised centuries before to Abraham and his descendants. It is only when the Greeks turn up that we come into the picture of God's eternal purpose that he was not only fulfilling his promise to Israel but more wonderfully he was reconciling the whole world to himself (2 Corinthians 5: 19). This is truly humbling.

Three words that obscure the origins of Christianity

It is deeply humbling to realize that Christianity concerns the identity and actions of Jesus, not the institutional fabric and traditions of the Western church. Jesus was a Jew and so were the apostles. The New Testament letters and texts were written overall by Jews and at least one Greek, Luke, who penned the gospel that bears his name and the sequel, the Acts of the Apostles. Nonetheless, Luke clearly understands the national context of the origins, identity, and mission of the Messiah, Jesus.

Christianity is primarily a faith about words, whereas the church is primarily a religion about power. Why do I say this? Is it not the case that James tells us that we need to put our words into action? (James 2: 26). It makes intuitive sense for James to say this. Anyone would know that people who do not *'practice what they preach,'* are hypocrites. One doesn't need to be a Christian to understand this. But Jesus is known as the embodiment of words, indeed John the apostle calls him the *'Word,'* or *'Logos'* in New Testament Greek. This is a profound statement, deeply controversial, and deeply significant. John says in the first verse of his account of the life of Jesus, *'in the beginning was the Word and the Word was with God and the Word was God. He was with God in the beginning.'*

John does not say *'in the beginning was power, true power,'* or *'in the beginning was wisdom,'* or *'in the beginning, was righteousness.'* I have pondered for years this most remarkable statement in John 1. Words matter. They matter because without words or language, or forms of communication, we cannot be understood. John is also identifying Jesus Christ with God and reflecting the language of the first book of the Bible, Genesis. In this enigmatic passage, God's words bring life. God says, *'let there be light and there was light'* (Genesis 1: 3). It is the uttering of God's words that brings about a life-changing transformation. God speaks and his speaking is power, his words change us, and his utterances transform matter. God needs only to speak, and the laws of physics are rent asunder. God needs only to speak and the world changes. The Devil or Diabolos was wrong and that is because Jesus did not need to turn stones into bread to prove his divine power. All he needed to do was speak, and lives were changed.

This is one of the reasons words are profoundly important. Our words are an echo of the Word of God, Jesus. Jesus as Logos, the God from ages past, the author of creation is the Word. Our words, being made in God's image, are simply echoes of him, faint, and fragile. Yet, our words do contain power and meaning and that is what words are. Anyone who has studied words or languages knows this. Words have meaning, not just for the conveying of information, but in the assessment of facts and the embodiment of meaning. Words, or the origin of words, are remarkable.

There are many words in the New Testament that have come to us today through the way the words are understood. There are slight variations, but the meanings have been retained. Four will suffice. The word we have today for something explosive is the word *'dynamite,'* which is related to the word *'dynamic'* which speaks of change or power, and the word dynamism, and so on. This comes from the Greek word *'dynamos'* which means power. The word we have as *'mystery'* which in English usually means something hidden comes from the Greek word *'mysterion'* which usually means something to be revealed. The word *'great'* is sometimes translated as *'mega,'* where we get mega-byte and so on. This comes from the Greek as well. The word *'Christ'* is not the surname of Jesus, but it is the Greek version of the word *'Messiah'* in Hebrew, the anointed one of God.

Words have power. The way to control words is to change them or change their meaning. The word of God is God's instrument in the world to convey his identity, nature, purpose, and character. It is no wonder that many have sought to interfere with the word of God for their own political, ideological, and economic purposes. The early Christians were a mixture of Jews and people from various nations in the ancient world. By the end of the first century and well into the second, fewer Jews came to faith in the Messiah Jesus. The parting of the ways had little to do with the person and identity of Jesus. Rather, it had to do with the attitudes towards the nature of the Jewish state and what to do with Rome. Christians refused to fight Rome and fled. The Jews lost their temple in AD 70 and were set to wander in a new nation-in-exile around the world, much like the wilderness wanderings of the people of Israel after their escape from bondage in Egypt.

Sadly, Christians decided to purge their assemblies of Jewish origins. They could not purge the original texts that they deemed to reflect the writings of the earliest apostles and testimonies, so they simply ignored them or used them to their own advantage. This new language of religion through the church replaced the spirit of Christianity, and through repetition, innovations became traditions, and new ideas became orthodoxy, and the Jewish and Biblical testimonies about Jesus became heresy. Three words define the Christian religion today. None are Biblical, none come from the Bible, and yet most Christians cannot speak for more than a minute without mentioning them. These words function as a form of propaganda, of indoctrination, and sadly, they speak nothing of God, and everything about people.

The first word is *'church.'* Most Christians need to say *'church'* regularly. It enables them to avoid mentioning God altogether. Most do. For most, the church is a place one attends weekly. The phrase *'my family and I go to church,'* is common. All that matters is that you attend, you turn up, you sit down, shut up, and do as you are told. Most Christians would insist that *'all Christians must go to church,'* or *'to be a Christian you must go to church.'* For Christians, *'church'* is where Christians gather, and only Christians who go to church can claim to follow Jesus. It is synonymous with Christianity. Jews have their synagogue and Christians have their church.

The problem is that the Bible disagrees with this. If *'assembly'* also means *'church,'* then the ancient Jews also had churches. Stephen, who was killed for speaking the truth to power (like John the Baptist), gave a speech just before he died (which was the cause of his death), recorded in the Acts of the Apostles. Luke includes a most remarkable admission. Luke records that Stephen said *'He (Moses) was in the assembly in the wilderness, with the angel who spoke to him on Mount Sinai, and with our ancestors; and he received living words to pass on to us' (Acts 7: 38).* Stephen is speaking about Moses who is gathered with the people of God at Sinai before he went up to get the Law, what we know as the great story of the Ten Commandments. The word Stephen uses for *'assembly'* in Greek, is the word we translate as *'church,'* which is *'ekklesia.'* Why is it not translated as *'church'* in English translations? It is not translated as *'church'* quite possibly because Christians want to make the statement that the *'church'* began with Peter and the apostles. It also embarrasses Christians because they mistranslate the word *'ekklesia'* throughout the New Testament. The use of the word *'church'* implies not a gathering of people around God, but a building built by men. If we wish to be consistent, the Hebrews who gathered around Moses at Sinai, were *'at church,'* but if this is the case, when did the *'church'* begin, was it with Abraham or with Peter? The West claims it is with Peter and the apostles, and that the Jewish believers in Christ and Hebrew testimony are irrelevant. The Bible makes no such arbitrary distinction. It is arbitrary, it is political, it is ideological, and sadly, it deprives Christians of fellowship with millions who testified to the Messiah they so eagerly claim to represent.

The word *'ekklesia'* indeed, has no religious connotation whatsoever. It simply means a gathering of people. It is non-sectarian and that is why the equivalent English meaning is ignored by the church. Churches want to make a statement, so everyone is clear about who is in and who is out, who is in the right and who is in the wrong. In Acts 19, the work of the apostle Paul leads to a riot in Ephesus (Acts 19: 23-41). In Acts 19: 41, the word *ekklesian* is translated as *'assembly,'* as it is in Acts 19: 39, and 19: 32. In this encounter, the *'church'* is not a gathering of Christians, but the people protesting and hating Paul for causing trouble in the city. The *'assembly'* in Acts 19 is gathering in a civic function in a secular context. Once again, if the word is the same in Greek, why don't we translate it as *'church'*?

The use of the word *'church'* in the New Testament is wrong. It doesn't arise from the text and bears no linguistic connection with New Testament Greek. There *is* an alternative English word, and that word is *'assembly.'* There is a final example of this mess in the New Testament from the book of Hebrews:

'Both the one who makes people holy and those who are made holy are of the same family. So, Jesus is not ashamed to call them brothers and sisters. He says, "I will declare your name to my brothers and sisters, in the assembly, I will sing your praises"' *(Hebrews 2: 11-12).*

The author is quoting Psalm 22: 22 and uses the word *'ekklesia'* in Greek. Again, if this means *'church,'* why is it not translated as *'church'* and why is the word *'assembly'* used in many modern translations? What it means is that churches existed in the Old Testament, during the time when the Jewish people looked forward to the coming of the Messiah. If we are to be consistent, Hebrews should read: *'in the church, I will sing your praises.'*

Furthermore, some of the most problematic verses in the New Testament are in Hebrews 12: 22-3.

'But you have come to Mount Zion, to the city of the living God, the heavenly Jerusalem. You have come to thousands upon thousands of angels in joyful assembly, to the church of the firstborn, whose names are written in heaven. You have come to God, the Judge of all, to the spirits of the righteous made perfect.'

Hebrews was most likely written in its original form before the fall of Jerusalem in AD 70, otherwise, it would speak of the temple in the past tense or omit mention of it entirely. For Jewish Christian readers, the participation of the nation of Israel is taken as a given, that the people who come to faith in Christ join those who testified to the Messiah, those who looked forward to his coming (Hebrews 11), but many Western Christians struggle with this because, according to them, Israel rejected the Messiah and the *'church'* began with the apostles and prophets (Ephesians 2: 20). What does *'joyful assembly'* mean in Greek? How about the *'church of the firstborn'*? In Greek, the word *'assembly'* in Hebrews 12 is mentioned only once in the entire New Testament. This unusual Greek word can mean a gathering or assembling of people for a festival, or a special event. The word *'church'* in *'church of the firstborn,'* also means *'assembly.'* If *'assembly,'* is a synonym, why not use it interchangeably with the word 'church' as an alternative reading?

The word *'church'* is found nowhere in the New Testament. It is probably from a much later Greek word to mean the House of God, a physical place that suited the transformation of Christianity into the national institutions that replaced multiethnic assemblies. Faith was replaced and usurped by the flag, and national churches were born. This was the creation of the church-state, the end of original

Christianity, and the rise of Christian Fascism, where people sought to emasculate God's power behind stone walls like a divine prison, with the wardens being a cadre of robed priests.

Nowhere in the New Testament is the *place* honored more than the *person*. The Gospel writers, Paul, and others make a deliberate and consistent break with the notion that God can be found in a place at all. Rather, anyone can know God, free of geographical constraints. The Ethiopian official can know Christ in his chariot beside the river (Acts 8: 26), a prison official in a prison (Acts 16: 30), or a divorced woman by a well (John 4). The New Testament abolishes the temple, or the need for a physical temple at least, as shown in the letter to the Hebrews. Sadly, once churches took over assemblies, in came the priests, the altars, the sacrifices, and the hideous evil of the Mass which is a *'Satanic Passover,'* a cruel parody and insult to the beauty of the Jewish rite as well as a mockery of the fellowship of faith in the Last Supper.

Christian Fascists demand church attendance and the quenching of the Spirit of God. They overturned Paul's teaching on the end of the ancient enmity between Jews and non-Jews. Today, the word *'church'* is meant to exclude Jews. It is unspoken Anti-Semitism, code for *'Jews are not welcome here.'* This is not the gospel, this is not Christianity, for anyone can join God's people; anyone can meet in the name of Jesus Christ and as Paul said, all are one in Christ, even Westerners.

The second word that is commonly used in the church but has no basis whatsoever in the Bible is *'priest.'* There are no priests in the New Testament. The only exception is the poetic license on the part of Peter who calls all those who believe in Christ, priests (1 Peter 2:5,9). This means that all Christians are priests, every one of them, as they are members of God's nation. This passage is an echo of Exodus where Moses writes in Exodus 19: 5-6, *'if you obey me fully and keep my covenant, then out of all nations, you will be my treasured possession. Although the whole earth is mine, you will be for me a kingdom of priests and a holy nation.'*

If you have an orthodox, Anglican, Catholic, or traditional background, then the man or woman exerting authority over you is a person without God's authority for there are no priests in the kingdom of God. The church invented the office of priests to exert power over people and keep them in servitude, poverty, and ignorance.

There are no priests in the kingdom of God, no office of priest in any of the lists of positions in any assembly, and none of the apostles, not even Peter, are referred to as priests. Many churches are set up like divine slaughterhouses which is what they are meant to be, places where the body of Christ is sacrificed whenever the priest says the incantations and prayers. The blasphemy of the Mass and the many horrid variations have at their center the idea that bread and wine magically turn into the body and blood of Christ. The word priest is used to destroy the power of God at work in the individual Christian, as well as the fellowship of all believers. It is also the mechanism for power and control and is the beating heart of this monied religion.

The only priest mentioned in the New Testament is Jesus Christ. Hebrews talks a lot about the position of the priest and the high priest in the Temple of Jerusalem and makes the comparison with Jesus Christ being the great high priest of God. Your local priest is probably still alive. Look for his wounds and his death on your behalf for sin, and you will find nothing. He or she, like you, needs a Savior. Like you, your priest needs to be set free and find peace. Like you, your priest is not God. Hebrews says:

Therefore, since we have a great high priest who has ascended into heaven, Jesus the Son of God, let us hold firmly to the faith we profess. For we do not have a high priest who is unable to empathize with our weaknesses, but we have one who has been tempted in every way, just as we are—yet he did not sin' (Hebrews 4: 14-15).

If your priest has died for you and ascended into heaven and sits at the right hand of God, I am sure he will be a priest, but as far as I know, only Christ could do that, and so that means your priest is dreadfully underqualified. You, and he, or she, are in the same boat.

Like the word *'church'* and *'priest,'* this final word is about detaching the church from Christianity and non-Jews from Jews. It is about trying to dispossess Jews from their homeland. The homeland of the Jews became the *'Holy Land'* which meant the land of Christians and not the land of Jews. They were not there anyway, having been expelled several times over the centuries. In Latin, the priests created the term *'Gentile'* which means in Latin, a nation, or a race. It is a generic term, so in Latin, the Jews as a nation could also be Gentile for in its meaning, Gentile does not mean non-Jewish. It is a strange word to apply to nations that are not Jewish. As the Latin language fell out of common use, why didn't Christians replace the word *'Gentile'* with the word *'nation'* or even *'race'*?

The purpose of the word *'Gentile'* is to deny the Jews a nation, or deny that they are a nation, and say instead they are simply a people or a wandering group of people without a nation. They have always been a nation, an ethnos, a people. The Gentiles are simply *'the other nations,'* the other peoples, the other ethnos. Israel did not become a nation first in 1948.

The Jews have always been a nation and they never ceased to be a nation simply because they had been expelled from the land of their ancestors. They were a nation when they wandered. They were a nation when they were in Babylon. A diaspora can also be a nation. A scattered people are still a people. Nationality and ethnicity are the same as far as the Bible understands it. Indeed, they are not a nation simply because they fit into the world of American Christian Fascists and their Middle East foreign policy strategy. Jews have maintained their identity down through the ages, as have many other ethnicities.

Why does any of this matter? It matters a great deal because Jesus was the Messiah of the Jews, not the nations. He came as the promised anointed one for Israel, the consolation of Israel. That is certainly how the Gospel writers and Paul saw it. Paul's letter to the Ephesians is confusing if we adopt the church's traditional view of expunging Jewishness from the text and read it as if the Jews did not exist. Modern Western Christians gloss over what they see as provincial and historical footnotes in the text, irrelevant to our identity in Christ if they can fit Jesus into the Culture War or their Christian Fascism. Instead of family and fellowship, Jews are seen as irrelevant, and antiquated, no longer central to the message of the gospel.

The opposite is true. Paul's writings show that non-Jews are brought in from far away only through the work of Christ. Paul writes in Ephesians 2 of all non-Jews, and that includes all Americans unless they are Jewish. I quote from the NIV (Ephesians 2: 11-13) which unfortunately retains the use of the word *'Gentiles.'*

'Therefore, remember that formerly you who are Gentiles by birth and called "uncircumcised" by those who call themselves "the circumcision" (which is done in the body by human hands)— remember that at that time you were separate from Christ, excluded from citizenship in Israel and foreigners to the covenants of the promise, without hope and without God in the world. But now in Christ Jesus, you who once were far away have been brought near by the blood of Christ.'

The purpose of God is to create a new humanity, a new people, a forgiven people, a holy people, who serve him, a people who know him and who are known by him. This essentially is what Ephesians is about. It is why Ephesians is such a radical and subversive book. It is no wonder many in the church hate it. Paul doesn't address his letter to the church. He addresses it to the *'saints in Ephesus and faithful in Christ'* (Ephesians 1: 1). These saints are people from Israel who believed in the Messiah. They were those who believe in Christ, the Messiah, those who were close by, by their historical position as the people of the covenant with God, the people of the promise. There were also non-Jews in Ephesus also called saints. Being a *'saint'* was simply a way of talking about someone who believed in Jesus. For those who are from the nations, this is grace upon grace, and once again, is deeply humbling. There is always in God's assembly, room for Jews who believe in Christ, after all, he is their Messiah. That assembly of believers in the risen Lord Jesus brought two different nations together in Christ.

We foreigners, before the coming of Christ, were *'excluded from citizenship in Israel and foreigners to the covenants of the promise, without hope and without God in the world.'* Interestingly, Paul mentions *'citizenship in Israel.'* The phrase is sometimes translated as *'Commonwealth of Israel,'* but Paul is speaking of citizenship, and it is a political term. Paul uses the Greek word *'politeias'* and there is no ambiguity in the meaning. Nor does Paul say that the nation of Israel is comprised only of people who lived in Palestine. He understood the ethnos of Israel, the people of Israel were spread out across the ancient world. He was from Turkey, the city of Tarsus. But he was still a Jew, he was still a citizen of Israel.

But due to the death of Christ, those of us who were far away were brought near. *'But now in Christ Jesus, you who once were far away have been brought near by the blood of Christ.'* Does this mean citizenship in Israel? Paul doesn't dwell on this here, though it is implied. Are not all one in Christ? The direction of all people who come to faith in Christ from the nations do not move towards America, or towards England, nor do they need to speak English to be close to God or understand God, nor do they need to wear Western clothes or have Western values. We are brought near to those to whom the promises, the covenant, and the Messiah were given, Israel.

What do the nations bring to God?

Is any nation better than another? What do the nations bring to God? Mercy is not mercy unless it is merciful. Grace is not grace unless it is given to one who needs it. In the Bible salvation, or the act of saving someone has no meaning unless one is saved from something to merit the saving in the first place. Forgiveness is pointless if one does not believe that one needs forgiveness. This is the problem of faith in a Western world that believes that simply being Western means being in a state of grace before God. The nation that proclaims, *'God bless America,'* presumes that America is already in a position of acquaintance with God, or fellowship with him, and on good terms. It is not faith that is assumed, but a right relationship with God.

Many of those who say *'God bless America'* are also, those who insist that other Americans need saving by the God in whom they already claim to place their trust. For the Christian Church, faith is something other people need, people outside the church, the sinners, the ones who do not go to church, who do not tithe to the church, who do not submit to the elders, or the priests, or the bishops, who do not obey the rules, and so on. There is therefore an uncomfortable paradox at the beginning of any discussion about the question of whether a nation has a special relationship with God.

Do *'Christian Nations'* have an advantage? The church overall believes that God began anew after the resurrection of Christ, that the church itself began with the apostle Peter and that the Jews, through their repudiation of the Messiah, forfeited their privileged position before God. They insist that the nation of Israel ceased to be after AD 70, but more importantly, the church was a clear break from the past, from the prophets and saints of the Hebrew Bible, and testimony. Nations that embraced the church could thus claim this privileged position in place of Israel, though some hold to the notion that one day Israel will, once again, become a nation. In America, the popular view is that this occurred in 1948. Before the return of Christ, these fortunate Jews have the chance to join the church, presumably American Christianity, for it tends to be Americans who hold to this perspective on the End Times. None of this thinking is in the New Testament.

Many in the West believe that they are Christians because they are Americans or Australians. Many white Australians, for example, believe being white is synonymous with being a Christian. *'I am Australian; therefore, I am a Christian.'* One hears statements like *'we live in a Christian country, with Christian values,'* which almost always means white values. For many who dare not stand up for their implicit white supremacy or racism as they did in the past, they wear the badge of *'Christian'* as code, a kind of *'nudge, nudge, wink, wink, you know what I mean,'* kind of political affiliation. In politics, the racists almost always identify as Christians, whereas the Christians in other parties tend to be more nuanced in their political identity. It is the same in America. There are many American Christians from Left to Right, but the ones who parade and celebrate their *'Christian values'* tend to be the ones who long for the *'good old days'* of white supremacy.

I hear phrases like *'Christian values are conservative values,'* *'Christian values are traditional values,'* or *'Christian values are family values.'* In Australia, the established church, or what's left of it, the Anglican Church, is intertwined with the monarchy of England, the educational institutions, the legal system, and the culture to such an extent that faith and flag are synonymous. More broadly, across the Anglo-Saxon nations, being in the West means being in a state of grace. Being a Westerner, one is closer to God or close to God.

In America, this attitude underpins in a deep cultural sense the philosophical background to the claim that America is a Christian nation, one that is blessed by God. It dates back to the time when a group of powerful slave owners had a soiree and decided to write their Constitution to enshrine a set of rights that applied only to them. The sad and pathetic revisionism that has occurred over the last century in America cannot dislodge the reality that these men were neither Christians, nor men of compassion, and the attempts of Christian Fascists to reconcile this monstrous document with Christianity have and will always fail. It continues to leave unresolved the tension between those who do not know God or care to know God and those who claim him as their own.

Central to this is the notion of being blessed by God is missionary work. The *'mission field'* is abroad, outside of the West, and all missionary agencies send their people abroad to the pagans, to the unbelievers. When I lived in Japan for a decade, the easiest visa to obtain for foreigners was the missionary visa and Sendai was crawling with missionaries. Some dared to present the good news of Jesus Christ, but most proclaimed America and American cultural values and could not tell the difference between flag and faith. For them, Jesus was white, he spoke English and the goal was to brainwash people and make them Americans. I have never met such a socially dysfunctional, ideologically unhinged, racist, ignorant class of people in my life. Fortunately, the Japanese politely ignore most of them, and they end up doing English-language weddings or English teaching.

At home in America or Australia, there is still the view that many in the West need saving, but it is lip service only. Few preach the gospel; most preach moralism of the kind Billy Sunday would be proud of. Christian Fascism is on the rise, and this comes with the view that the West is Christian, under attack from enemies foreign and domestic. Bible college graduates claw each other's eyes out to get on the short-list for the best vacation spots, I mean the best mission locations such as France, Germany, the Bahamas, Hawaii, and Venice. After all, those surfers need the gospel, as do the wealthy and filthy rich which explains why in Sydney, evangelicals love church-planting in the wealthiest suburbs. In some wealthy suburbs, there are more church plants than coffee shops. Mission work is an industry now, a superb lifestyle to the fortunate few who manage to get it, a life of ease, of *'coffee evangelism'* or *'beach evangelism.'* It is driven by the belief that God has set up his home in the West, that God is here, and that he sends his people to the darkest corners of the world.

The phrase *'deepest, darkest Africa,'* is still used in Australian

Christian circles, even though there are more African Christians than the entire population of that tiny land down under. Missionary agencies still send people abroad to *'save the heathen,'* while most at home are not Christians. The latest Census (2021) is devastating. Anglicanism is on the verge of extinction, while most other denominations are one foot in the grave already.

Despite this astounding reality, many Western Christians are deeply offended if Chinese or Japanese or Korean, or African missionaries turn up to preach the gospel to them. God forbid. During America's invasion of Iraq, following the missiles and the war crimes were the missionaries with their version of American Christianity, ever eager to tell people about the white Jesus, those who were not blown to bits. I remember one story of an American pastor astounded that there was a Christian community in Iraq that has been there for centuries. According to the new evangelists, they were not true Christians of course, they did not worship God in English, nor did they speak English, and were not Protestants.

What do the nations bring to God? We bring nothing of value to God. Nothing. We bring nothing he can use. We bring nothing that can impress him. Christian Fascists do not get it. They think that being born in the West is a positive point as if God picks favorites based on criteria we deliver to him. Also, they think that church attendance counts for something. They think that a good life counts for everything. None of it does.

The West however is so deeply arrogant. This arrogance is ingrained in our culture. The life of a person in the West is worth more in our eyes than someone not born here. We generally look down on the rest of the world as inferior. National sins are the things other nations have, not us. If we do, then we know whom to blame. It is never us. We see this in the myopic attitude to the war in Ukraine. Most Western people have no idea where Ukraine is but are deeply concerned about the war. There are wars in Africa such as in Ethiopia and wars in the Middle East such as in Yemen. The West could not care less about these other wars because they do not involve white people. The life of a child in Yemen is not as important as a Ukrainian child. Every night, churches pray for Ukraine and weep and rail against Putin, but who cries for the children of Yemen? God apparently will still bless us if we turn away from suffering in parts of the world we don't care about. This is disgraceful theology.

The attitude seems to be that since we are Americans, we already have one foot in heaven. Our Western values say that we are good enough for God, after all, I have heard so many luminaries announce in recent years that *'we are the greatest nation in the history of the world.'* It is an incredible statement. This intellectual disease I have begun hearing in Australian circles too, which is even more remarkable. It seems, from our point of view that we don't need God, in fact, he needs us, and in fact, he is lucky to know us.

But encountering God means that none of that counts for anything. It is a place of deep humility, where we can bring nothing of virtue or goodness to God. Nothing impresses him. Nothing wins him over. Not even his love for us. His love is wishful thinking outside his love in action, which was the death of Christ for sin. The greatest act of God was to do something we could not do, and that is deal with the problem of sin, which is rebellion against the kingship of God. It is impossible for us to overcome this inner weakness of spirit and heart, though many have tried. God sent Jesus to stand for us, in our stead, so that where we could not stand, he stood, he fought for us, and he died for us, and everything that we need to know about God concerns God and his relationship with us. The starting point for faith is not us, it is God, and the answer is not us, it is God.

If there was anyone who loved his nation, it was the apostle, Paul. He was a great nationalist, a man who truly loved his people and his nation. But it was Paul, the Jewish nationalist, who wrote much about the relationship between faith and flag. Indeed, his writings are the textbook for our understanding of what many see as critical to understanding faith in our world today. I refer to his letter to the Ephesians, penned probably around the early 60s AD. Paul brings us some home truths about where we in the nations stand before God. He explains the relationship between faith and flag.

Paul was the man, or one of them, who felt a conviction to bring the message, the evangelion (which is where we get the word evangelism) to the nations, those nations who were not, and are not, Israel. It is a slap in the face; it really is. This certainly brings us down a few notches. I dare you to read Ephesians. It is the cure for Christian Fascism, or Christian Nationalism, which convinces me that most fascists have never read the Bible, or if they do, they ignore what is said there. There are no grounds for our confidence outside the grace of God found in Jesus. There are no grounds for our confidence to be found in our nation, our history, our skin color, or our background. Those who say that there is such confidence are liars, and yes, that includes priests, ministers, pastors, bishops, and popes.

In Ephesians, Paul is speaking to us, and probably to most of you. It is how we were, it was our lives, it was our condition. What do we have to offer God, those of us from the nations? Paul says we bring nothing of value to God. The first thing Paul tells us is that we were dead before God. Dead. He says: *'As for you, you were dead in your transgressions and sins' (Ephesians 2:1).*

It means lifeless, mortal, without life. This means we had no life, no spiritual life before God. The word he uses is *'nekros'* which is where we get many words. It means death. He does not mean physical death but spiritual. Our death is because of our trespasses and sins, both used in the plural sense, and inclusive sense in that all of us in the nations once were dead in this way. Paul speaks in a general, comprehensive sense. Our sins and our trespasses bring us death. All of us. Without exception. All people in the nations are dead because of both. What is the difference between the two? Sin in Greek refers to missing the mark, guilt, failure, the idea of shooting an arrow and not hitting the target, the idea of falling short of not finishing, or not fulfilling. Trespasses mean a falling away, a slip, a misstep, and so on.

Christian Fascists tell you that certain sins place you in various positions regarding others in their kingdom. Some people are better than others. They will tell you that being born in America or Australia or the West counts for something. This is not how the Bible reads, and it is not how Paul thought. Paul believed in real equality before God. To use a colloquial phrase, we are all in the same boat. We are all in this together.

Paul doesn't stop there. He presents a vision of the world that is deeply disturbing. It is disturbing because of the phrase *'all of us,'* and because the starting point for all people is so depressingly awful. Paul writes in Ephesians 2: 1-4:

'As for you, you were dead in your transgressions and sins, in which you used to live when you followed the ways of this world and

of the ruler of the kingdom of the air, the spirit who is now at work in those who are disobedient. All of us also lived among them at one time, gratifying the cravings of our flesh, and following its desires and thoughts. Like the rest, we were by nature deserving of wrath.'

Surely, the Bible got it wrong. The West is Best, right? This is not the kind of message that affirms the nations. It is not the kind of message that elevates the nations such as Rome or Greece, or America. We bring nothing to God. While we were dead, we walked or followed in the ways of the world. This *'following'* was not after God, but after the spirit who works in all people, presumably the Devil, though he is not mentioned by name.

This is strong stuff. This is Paul surveying the nations, the so-called Christian nations today, America, Britain, and Australia. You bring nothing to God. Nothing. You walk according to the Devil, you follow evil, and you are dead. It is not simply an action here or an action there, a misplaced thought or an innocent failing. It is not ticking one of the boxes on the Christian Fascist *'sin list,'* it is a lifestyle, a way of life, it is every day, all day, not just one sin or being caught in a sin, but it is being consumed by sin. The result is simple in Paul's mind – by nature deserving of wrath, which simply means God's destruction. So much for America or the West or any nation that exists today or did exist.

What Paul is saying is that nations have a starting point of zero. What of the nations? In God's eyes, outside of the Messiah, they are dead. All of them. Dead. That is not the news people want to hear. Surely being an American, counts? Surely being a Westerner counts? No. The one who brings life is God and he has no favorites.

Are certain nations blessed by God?

One of the greatest lies of Western Christianity is that the nations of Britain and America are closer to God than other nations. This was certainly at the heart of Western imperialistic logic during the Victorian Era for Britain and the post-war American era of exceptionalism.

Christians in these nations are often very proud of their nations, hoisting flags in their churches, singing nationalist hymns, and often aligning their national enterprise with the will and purpose of God. To be an Englishman in the nineteenth and early twentieth century was to be a *'Civilized Christian Man,'* a man who knew how to speak, how to eat, how to dress, and how to live. He knew his place in society, he knew how to sing the hymns of God in the right chords and with the right intonation of tone, and accent, he knew that God only accepted worship in the spirit of holiness and awe, with organ music, and Sunday best, and upstairs-downstairs. He was most certainly a man. Women were at home, and children were to be seen and not heard. Those outside the wealthy parts of society were oppressed and living in misery. The church saw no problem with these racial and class distinctions, though there were always a few crazy people of faith in every generation who tried to bring some consistency between public Christianity and the Bible.

To be a Christian for most missionaries was to be white, it was to live up to white standards, adopt white ways, and sing the praises of what we now call *'white supremacy.'* To become a Christian, everyone was forced to give up their cultural values, background, their customs, and traditions, and become copies of white people. It is impossible to understand the British Empire and American culture up till the 1970s without acknowledging the complicity and advocacy of the church of white supremacy.

For Britain, it was the heyday of British Christian Fascism, the glory days, the days of the Empire. These days, the descendants of these cultural cockroaches are scurrying up and down the Culture Wars, literally whitewashing history, writing books expunging the vile truths of church complicity in racism, genocide, and cultural imperialism, while their church buildings are falling due to rot, mildew, and rising damp. They demand more and more money from the state to preserve an institution that should be torn down to remove the stain of a history that needs only to be remembered in history books and not seen on every street corner. The best churches in Britain now are museums, flower shops, or cafes, and strangely enough, many of these new proprietors seem to know how to tend, care for, and preserve these beautiful cultural landmarks more than those who went every Sunday to worship a God they pretended to believe in. Certainly, up until the end of the Second World War, many churches in America, Britain, and Australia excluded the poor as they practiced 'pew rentals' for the rich, where families bought seats in church.

Paul, writing 2,000 years ago would be astonished at the claims of the West and their alleged intimacy with the Almighty and he might have had a thing or two to say about it. He would have been on the side of those who are calling for an end to white supremacy. He would throw his hands up in despair and maybe reach for the whip he once spoke of, but after reading many of his letters for many years now, I believe the stupidity and the arrogance of the West would produce in the great apostle a stunned silence and then prayer that God would not immediately destroy those who so arrogantly place themselves on the throne of God.

For Paul, these white nations of Europe are just other nations, among the family of ethnos or other nations, outside of the nation of Israel, which has always existed since Abraham. Paul writes:

'Remember...that at that time you were without Christ, alienated from the Commonwealth of Israel and strangers of the covenants of promise, having no hope and without God in the world' (Ephesians 2: 12).

These are harsh words for the British Empire, for America, for the white man and white woman. The nations are without Christ, without hope, without God in the world. They have their ways and their cultures, and their beliefs, but they do not have God. They have no hope. The only hope came from Israel, for through Israel came the Messiah. For Paul, the message of the gospel, the good news about Jesus is real because it is the only hope for the nations. It is not that the Christian *'good news'* can add a little something to the British or American culture and add a little bit of God or change a little, but this is the message that changes everything and without it, there is no hope. Paul writes:

'But now in Christ Jesus, you who were then far off came to be near by the blood of Christ...And coming he preached peace to you, the ones afar off, and peace to the ones near' (Ephesians 2: 13, 17).

The one that brought us close to God was not a nation, was not an idea, a war, or a philosophy. It was a person, and for Christians, this person is Jesus, the Messiah, or the Christ, as the Greeks would call him. Through his sacrificial death on the cross, Jesus reached out, across the vastness of the world, beyond his own people, and found all those that his Father would give him, those who wander, those who are lost, those who seek, those who despair, those who yearn for freedom, and he saved them. He saved them because they were far away, and he saved them because he was the only one who could bring them near, and he was the only one who could bring peace because he was the only one who could die for other people.

The nations were far away from God, outside of Israel. The ones who are far off, are the nations, and the ones close or near is the nation of Israel. Both are brought to God by the blood of Christ. It is not just the nations, that are outside of Israel, but also Israel and the Jews. There is equality. Strange as it may seem in a culture that is deeply Anti-Semitic, the fact is that salvation is possible, even for the Gentiles, even for the nations, even for those far off, as much as it is for the Jews, the ones with the covenants of promise.

The reality of faith for Paul, writing in that first generation, as a Jew who encountered the risen Christ is that the good news that was for Israel was also for the nations. The early Christians, many of whom were Jews, struggled with the idea that salvation was also for the nations. Paul, the evangelist to the nations, took this message, that the nations could find peace with God through Jesus Christ. It was through Christ that both could find God the Father, both could find peace, and both enjoy the fellowship of being in this new family or household of God. Paul writes:

'For he is our peace, he is making us both one, and breaking down the middle wall of partition, annulling in his flesh the enmity, the Laws of commandments and decrees that he might in himself create the two into one new man, making peace, and might reconcile both in one body to God through the cross, slaying the enmity in himself' (Ephesians 2: 14-16).

Christ brought Jews and non-Jews together as equals. The main purpose of Paul's letter is to show that in Christ, both those of the nation of Israel and the other nations are brought together as one. The tragedy is not that Jews and non-Jews are often separate now, that happened later, but the tragedy is that among the nations, there is no equality before God in Christ. For centuries, nations and

Christians within nations outdo each other to create division. Wealth divides the church; position divides the church, and the West has made it a mantra that race or ethnicity divides the church. In the Church today, nationality is everything. You may be a Christian, but all that matters is where you were born, which denomination you support, and which side you take.

Like Marxists who grieved for the working class who butchered each other on the Somme doing the bidding of the nations, I grieve for Christianity trapped within national Christian Fascism, where faith is added to the flag, often literally. But it is skin-deep and does not change the human heart. This is not surprising because the best that church baptism can do is put water on the skin for a few moments until the air dries it off, but the baptism of God that comes through true faith in Jesus changes the heart. This is a language the church does not understand even now, even after centuries of the Bible, which most churches keep closed for fear that people might find out about God and more importantly discover that the church has lied to them from the beginning.

For Christian Fascists in the West, there is no problem with faith and flag being bosom buddies. For generations, white people were at the top and the rest were underneath them. This is a repudiation of the Gospel, and it means in practice that many so-called Christians in the last two centuries were simply not people who followed Christ. I doubt very much that any or many of the missionaries who took the white man's gospel to the heathen knew anything about the gospel of Jesus Christ, they were there for themselves, they lorded their position over others, and Christians in many churches have spent the last generation trying to undo the terrible damage done to the people for whom Christ came.

Sadly, many mission agencies are deeply entrenched with white supremacy, and many missionaries today are the same as those who went with pith helmets, tight shorts, and heavy clothes, only they walk with tight mouths, angry eyes, and clenched fists. One said to me in Kyoto of the Japanese *'Satan has all of them around his little finger.'* Amazingly, she knew the hearts of all 126 million Japanese, but it might have been better if she knew even basic language skills.

But it was not simply Jesus who was the one who brought people together. He brought them together for a purpose, a more radical idea and that was to create a new assembly of people drawn from all nations, a new humanity, a new spiritual temple of the Holy Spirit, not built with bricks, or mortar, or defined by nationality or passport, but by the Spirit. Paul writes (Ephesians 2: 18-22):

'For through him, we both have access to the Father by one Spirit. Consequently, you are no longer foreigners and strangers, but fellow citizens with God's people and also members of his household, built on the foundation of the apostles and prophets, with Christ Jesus himself as the chief cornerstone. In him, the whole building is joined together and rises to become a holy temple in the Lord. And in him, you too are being built together to become a dwelling in which God lives by his Spirit.'

Fellow citizens, members of his household, and a holy temple. This is a remarkable assertion by Paul, and it is a pity the church ignores it. It is not hundreds of temples, nor are temples defined by national or ethnic boundaries. God lives among his people, and he lives among all his people in the same way and the same fashion. As with everything Paul says, there are no favorites with God.

Even non-Jews can join the household of God, even Americans! God's people Paul mentions are the saints, those Jewish Christians whom both believed in the Messiah and those who looked forward to the coming of the Messiah. Even the nations are no longer strangers to God but are brought into the household of God, not the church, not the buildings, not the Roman Catholic Church or the Orthodox Church, or whatever, but God's people, Israel. This is confirmed by the presence not only of the apostles but the prophets, the men of the Hebrew Bible who taught the coming of the Messiah, and this includes John the Baptist and Simeon and others.

Paul is adamant that God does not save nations, but he saves people from all nations. The goal of the coming of the Messiah is not to create a new nation called Britain or America or Australia, but a new humanity in Christ, a dwelling of God where God lives by his Holy Spirit. This is not any nation, nor is it exclusively a nation, or your nation. No nation around today comes anywhere near this ideal.

Christian Fascism, therefore, that seeks to link the nation with God is entirely and utterly a corrupt and evil enterprise with no basis in the Bible. It should be exposed for the complete fraud that it is. Faith and flag do not belong together. For Americans, it is time to put aside that unbiblical notion of *'God and the Constitution.'* God did not write the American Constitution, men did. God is not the author of the American Constitution. More importantly, as a Christian, the Constitution of any nation is not of the same caliber as the Bible. You cannot compare the writing inspired by the Spirit of God and the ramblings of men who kept slaves and believed that might was right. God does not take sides. All people everywhere from all nations can have the Spirit can have God dwelling with all of them, equally with the one Lord and Savior and one hope found in Christ.

Do nations have a divine destiny?

Do nations have a divine destiny? Nowhere does the New Testament give any nation a destiny. The nations are simply the vast pool of humanity from which God will draw his lost sheep, his children, his people, and those who follow his Son, Jesus the Messiah. The purpose of the nations is simply that, that they are the ones who will hear the message about Jesus, respond, believe in Jesus, and receive the Spirit of God.

Out of the nations, including the nation of Israel (which has always been a nation, not simply a people), God creates a new people, his people, a new nation. Peter, a Jew, a fisherman, and a disciple of Jesus, who was by no means a perfect man, speaking to those who followed Christ throughout the ancient world, said this in 1 Peter 2: 9-11:

'But you are a chosen people, a royal priesthood, a holy nation, God's special possession, that you may declare the praises of him who called you out of darkness into his wonderful light. Once you were not a people, but now you are the people of God; once you had not received mercy, but now you have received mercy.'

These are disturbing words, especially one phrase if you are a Christian Fascist: *'once you were not a people, but now you are the people of God.'* This is the most offensive phrase to Christian nationalists and Christian Fascists. Listen if you are a Christian Fascist:

'You were not a people before you knew God, you lived in the nations, but you had nothing to bind you together, your ties were of no significance whatsoever, and you did not know God. When God called you out of darkness, he called people from all nations, including people from nations you despise, with colors you spit on, with ethnicities you condemn, with backgrounds you look down upon, with names you deliberately mispronounce, with cultures you scorn, and they are your equals before God. They are not inferior to you, they are not lesser than you, and you are no better than them because you are all called not into the light of your nation or your culture or your language but into the light of Christ. You become God's people only because of the mercy of God.'

Unfortunately, we live in a world where nations believe that they have a destiny. If Christians believe in God, then nations must, in this view, have a divine destiny. This national belief has become an obsession to the point where many Christians, who claim to believe in Jesus Christ, cannot tell the difference between nationalism and faith. It is not just America. This sickness is everywhere now. This madness is commonplace and I do believe it is one of the greatest threats to liberal democracy today.

Many social commentators call this *'Christian nationalism'* and I beg them not to. You must stop using the term because it is wrong. There is nothing wrong with nationalism. It is simply a love of one's nation and there is nothing wrong with that. We must love something, and nations are among the building blocks of our society. They are ancient categories.

I use the term Christian Fascism for that locates the essential nature of their beliefs – the use of the state to force people to adopt so-called *'Christian values,'* none of which are Christian. This form of politics is misery and oppression. Anyone of any creed or belief must oppose them. Christian Fascism is a cancer in the West and increasingly in the East. Call these Christian Nationalists by their true name, expose their true identity, and reveal their true allegiance. They are fascists. They use Christianity to advance their own political and economic agendas.

But it is not only Christian Fascists that are on the destiny bandwagon. Many secularists hold to the notion of exceptionalism, the idea that America is special, unique, all-powerful, with a special purpose in the world and world history. They hold to a broader notion of God, a broader conception of the divine. Many Christians also seem to think that anyone who talks about God must be a Christian. This is a secular deification of the state, unlike anything we have seen in the past. The British said, *'God save the Queen,'* while some Americans deify the nation and say: *'God bless America.'* Hungary and Poland are other nations that are calling for a return to the past, a revival of so-called *'Christian'* values, even in Australia, once a secular society, the sickness of Christian Fascism is rising, strangling politics, and killing faith.

But what if nations do not have a destiny? What if nations are entirely free? What if God has given them free reign in the world? Of course, I believe that God orders all things according to his providence or his guiding hand through the course of events and people. This is the idea that God works through us. Much of it is a mystery, as to why or how things are done. After all, we are not God.

The Bible gives us a clue. In the first book of the Hebrew Bible, Joseph, who was sold into slavery by his brothers reflected on this for many years. At the end of his life, he could tell his brothers, you guys meant it for evil, but God meant it for God (Genesis 50: 20). Such incredible words. Incredible. Only a man who has suffered terrible pain could ever say those words. He admits the wrong, the crime, the evil, but he sees, also the divine hand of God at work, in his life, and in the lives of his brothers. They meant it for evil, but God meant it for good.

Then we have Christ himself and his terrible death on the cross. Peter says to the crowd of men, a few days after the cross, many of whom were in the mob who called for the death of Jesus, that evil men put him to death, but he also died due to the predetermination and election of God (Acts 2: 23). Peter said: *'This man was handed over to you by God's deliberate plan and foreknowledge; and you, with the help of wicked men, put him to death by nailing him to the cross.'* (NIV). Christians get so much in a muddle over this verse and seem to have no problem with what Joseph said, but both men are saying the same thing. This is because God works through human agency in mysterious ways to accomplish his purposes. It is man's intent, but God's purpose.

God's purpose concerns his Son. What if God has no purpose for nations? What if nations are here for one purpose and one purpose alone? In addition, what if that purpose has nothing to do with them? What if all nations are simply gathered for one reason, and one reason alone, what then? Well, first there would be profound readjustment. Profound. Nations with destiny would realize their entire reason for being was a lie, a deceit. There may even be something we used to call humility. Do you see humility in the current American Culture War? I see lots of anger, lots of hatred, lots of protests, accusations, name-calling, slander, and threats – and that's just in the church.

Paul says this about all those who follow Jesus. It is his exhortation or advice. Check your hearts to see if you measure up, or see these qualities in your nation, or national leadership (Ephesians 4: 2-3):

'Be completely humble and gentle; be patient, bearing with one another in love. Make every effort to keep the unity of the Spirit through the bond of peace.'

Is that American politics today or the face of American foreign policy? Is America known for its humility? What do you think?

Paul tells us that he believes *'the nations'* have no destiny. He would laugh at the Christian Fascists and their mad American dream of a Christian nation and call it all complete nonsense. America is simply another nation. Whether it was founded 300 years ago by the slave traders and warmongers and puritans or whether it was formed by the many first nation peoples, they are simply a nation or a set of nations, like all nations. Paul of course wrote 2,000 years ago. He never went to America, but the point is, no nation, no set of nations, has a purpose. People have a purpose, but nations don't.

The Bible is silent on the mechanics of nations. What fascists don't tell you is that the Hebrew Bible is written primarily for the Jewish nation, and so the rhetoric about national righteousness, obedience, and blessings does not concern America in the twenty-first century, but ancient Israel. The Psalms were liturgical pieces for worship in Solomon's temple which was destroyed by Babylon. The prophecies of Ezekiel, Isaiah, and Jeremiah were for a people in Exile, a wandering people, a lost people, and a people seeking to find certainty in a world where they had lost everything. It is impossible to read the great prophets in the Hebrew Bible without the context of deep mourning, sadness, regret, and expectation.

Paul's thinking repudiates exceptionalism entirely. Paul is interested in Jesus Christ, how to know him, grow in him, and how to follow him. He is not interested in *Politics 101*. His thinking pushes us back to the original schools of thought in secular education that challenge us to see all nations the same. If you want to know the mechanics of the state, then go to liberalism, Marxism, or realism, but do not go to the Bible. It is silent. It is completely silent. Why don't we hear this more often? Because the Christian Fascists in America lie about the Bible all the time. They rarely open it, and when they do, they ignore what is written there. They pick and choose verses from obscure prophets in the Hebrew Bible and apply them to America and talk about destiny. Paul writes:

'To me, the least of all the saints this grace was given to preach the message in the nations, the unsearchable riches of Christ, and to bring all to light what is the fellowship of the mystery having been hidden from eternity in God, the one creating all things through Jesus Christ that might be made known now to the rulers and the authorities in the heavens through the assembly the manifold wisdom of God, according to the eternal purpose which he accomplished in Christ Jesus our Lord' (Ephesians 3: 8-11).

I can promise you that few Christian leaders in America will touch these verses because Paul takes a sledgehammer to national pride. There is no national throne alongside God, for Christ stands there. The great mystery is not humanity but God, it is not the riches on earth, but the riches of knowing Christ, it is not human authorities that needed to be notified, but heavenly ones. Earthly authorities and powers were simply ignored as unimportant. The mystery was *'made known now to the rulers and the authorities in the heavens,'* not to Rome or Israel, or even America. Paul demolishes national pride. There is nothing left. He smashes it. All of it. It is broken into a thousand pieces. And so, it should be. The focus is Jesus, it is not the church, and it is not any nation.

There are three ideas I would like to draw out from Paul's rather enigmatic statement. First, the problem of the translation of *'church'* and *'saints.'* Paul is not talking about the church, he is speaking of the assembly, a gathering of people who are those who testify about the unsearchable riches of Christ. The *'saints'* are not good people or people that are elevated by the church, but all people from Abraham onwards who looked forward to the arrival of the Messiah, as well as the many Jewish people who accepted Christ as their Messiah. They are also the people from the nations who have come to faith in Jesus. Paul even calls himself *'the least of all the saints,'* which suggests that sainthood is not bestowed by the Pope.

Second, the *'mystery that was hidden from eternity in God'* is one concerning fellowship, which means friendship, communion, and brotherhood. This is the assembly of believers drawn from those who come from the nation of Israel who believes in Jesus, and from the nations who believe in Christ, and they are all members of the same assembly.

Third, the *'eternal purpose of God'* is Jesus, not America, it is the assembly of men and women drawn from Israel and the nations that exhibit the wisdom of God. This assembly of people is the eternal purpose of God that was accomplished in Christ Jesus. This eternal purpose was shaped by the Messiah. This is an assembly, a group of people drawn from the nations, not the nations themselves, and the only purpose of God is his wisdom to create a new humanity centered on the person of Jesus Christ.

Christianity is about Christ and our relationship with him. It is not about America, its values, and future. There is one new humanity in Christ. The new humanity has nothing to do with the nation, there is no connection between the gospel and the nation, and there is no Christian nation. The nation is significant only as a place where the gospel is preached, and people are drawn from the nations to join God's assembly exhibiting the manifold wisdom of God. Membership in this assembly is not about religion, baptism, denominations, or nations, but simply a new humanity centered on Jesus Christ. Fear comes from nations that believe they have a destiny, but the Bible teaches they do not. None of them do. Their pride in themselves has the result of filling them with fear that others will seek to take away their power. They transfer this fear onto you so that you are anxious and under their control.

The nations have no destiny. They are free. God has set them free in Christ, who is available to all. You are free as well. Fear need not control you. Christ has come to set us free from fear, anxiety, and despair so that through the light of God's word, we might experience the unsearchable riches of Christ and walk each day in freedom.

3   THE LIE OF FREE SPEECH

There is no such thing as free speech

One of the great lies of liberal democracy is free speech. It is a lie for so many reasons. I will not spend too much time proving this as it is so obvious. Speech is not *'free.'* It is often costly. What we say has consequences. The old proverb *'sticks and stones may break my bones, but names will never hurt me,'* is at best wishful thinking, or at worst license to abuse.

Being the victim of racial epithets for example, or being criticized because of our shape or size, skin color or temperament, family background or postal address, are all examples of how words hurt. Words can tear, words can wound, and they can kill. If you do not believe me, talk to the parents of the many children who have committed suicide due to verbal bullying at school. In Japan, for example, they even have this hideous thing called *'silent death'* where people act as if someone doesn't exist. The goal is for that person to kill themselves. Everyone pretends the victim is dead out of the hope that it becomes a reality. I know. I was once on the receiving end of this venom. It does not matter the age. Words or the absence of words can be destructive, but especially for young children or vulnerable people, words can be catastrophic. Free speech is a lie.

With our words we can hurt, insult, verbally maim, slander,

assault, undermine, demolish, and discourage. What we say has been given so much attention by our Lord and his apostles that the phrase *'free speech is not free'* can be amply proved by recourse to a variety of texts in the New Testament and Hebrew Bible. I could go on all day, but the place to go is the letter written by James. James was the brother of Jesus, and much of his letter reads like someone who grew up with Jesus or was certainly acquainted with his style. James said:

'Likewise, the tongue is a small part of the body, but it makes great boasts. Consider what a great forest is set on fire by a small spark. The tongue also is a fire, a world of evil among the parts of the body. It corrupts the whole body, sets the whole course of one's life on fire, and is itself set on fire by hell. All kinds of animals, birds, reptiles, and sea creatures are being tamed and have been tamed by mankind, but no human being can tame the tongue. It is a restless evil, full of deadly poison' (James 3: 5-8).

What we say, says James, can corrupt the entire body and can send us to Hell. These are strong words. Our tongue is *'a restless evil, full of deadly poison.'* How true. James has been to church. Well, he spent time around people, even people who claimed to be godly and holy, and righteous. He must have been to church! I often say that people do not go to church these days, because they know the people who do.

Behind this proverb of mine is the reality that much of church life has to do with gossip, slander, character assassination, and just general bile and criticism. It is my experience that church people are often judgmental people with a judgmental spirit. It is not long before they pass judgment on you for something. Try to have a conversation with a religious person and speak normally. Use a stopwatch and see how long it is before they pass judgment on you for something especially if you open your mouth and start talking about God.

Interestingly, James makes a most startling comment. I had to read it a few times just to make sure I was not misreading it. He says it a few verses earlier in his letter, as he begins his tirade, shall we say, against the misuse of words in the early Christian community in Israel and the nations: *'We all stumble in many ways. Anyone who is never at fault in what they say is perfect, able to keep their whole body in check.' (James 3:2).* What this means is that someone who never transgresses in the words they use, or what they say, is a perfect or complete person able to control or restrain their complete body. The word *'control'* simply means to lead with a bridle, like riding a horse. It suggests discipline. It suggests something learned. It makes sense since speech is a learned behavior. The control of speech must be too.

This is a remarkable verse of scripture. We should put this on our cell phone or laptop or iPad or Chrome book. Remember, James, the brother of Jesus, the leading light in the little Jerusalem assembly that met in the Temple Courts is most likely the author. He was martyred for his faith in Jesus Christ:

'We all stumble in many ways. Anyone who is never at fault in what they say is perfect, able to keep their whole body in check' *(James 3:2).*

James is admitting that he and his readers are the same. He stumbles and he stumbles in many ways. What an honest, humble reflection. He didn't say: *'you stumble in many ways, you sinners, not like me.'* He wasn't a Christian Fascist. Acts portray him as an ambiguous leader, trying to keep a balance between the various factions, Jews, and non-Jews. But here, he identifies with everyone. James was a disciple of Christ. We all are. We are all the same. Do not put anyone up on a pedestal especially not those who claim to be Christian leaders. Christians often do this. We put people up as perfect and don't realize that we are all just followers of Jesus. (If you don't believe me, just look up the last verse of the Psalmist's longest Psalm 119, and read what that says). We all stumble in many ways.

In Greek, the word for stumbling also means to sin, transgress or be in error. It comes from the word trip or fall. The Greek word means to trespass so why is it not mentioned as such? I think the translators are uncomfortable with the idea that Christians can transgress often, so they use a more polite word *'stumble.'* It does not fit with the assumption that Christians are *'righteous'* or *'holy'* people. This suggests that maybe James might agree that Romans 7 describes a Christian perspective. To confirm this, James points out that this stumbling is not occasional, but often, and *'many.'* But James goes further. He not only points out that there is no such thing as free speech, but he also busts that other terrible myth: *'words don't matter, only actions do.'* Nowhere does the Bible make this assertion. It is completely wrong. What we say matters. Words are never cheap. James says: *'Anyone who is never at fault in what they say is perfect, able to keep their whole body in check' (James 3:2).*

A person who can control their tongue and attitude has got it together. That is what he is saying. Words do matter. Words have power, they can hurt, but they can also cause trouble. They often do. For reasons which to me are not entirely clear, many people who go to church are unaware of the legal implications of slander or libel. Furthermore, they seem to believe that slander, gossip, malicious or otherwise, is like *'parliamentary privilege.'* This is the belief that if you slander someone in parliament, then you are free from legal action. This is not true of course. It is entirely possible that a member of parliament can be sued for slander for what they say publicly even in the chambers of state. In the church, there is not even parliamentary privilege, but many Christians believe that being a Christian means that you must forgive a slanderer or gossip, or a malicious liar and conversely you possess as a believer in Jesus, absolute freedom to slander others. The apostles point out that gossip and slander are a sin and an evil and those who practice both in Church and enjoy it, are most likely those without faith in God at all.

Slander existed in all Christian communities, destroying the testimony of Christ from the very beginning of the gatherings. Slander and gossip are also terrible sins and are condemned throughout the New Testament as signs of unbelief and apostasy (Matthew 15: 19, Mark 7: 22, Romans 1:30, 1 Corinthians 5:11, 1 Corinthians 6: 10, 2 Corinthians 12:20; Ephesians 4:31, Colossians 3:8, 2 Timothy 3:3, Titus 3: 2, James 4:11, 1 Peter 2:1). True Christians do not gossip or slander. That is a pity because it means that many church-going people are not Christians!

It is the tragedy of the modern Christian Church in the West that it is often a cesspool of slander and gossip. If Christian people cannot find dirt on someone they don't like, they will just make it up. The lives of many people in the church are regularly destroyed by slander and gossip. Curiously, the church courts are generally not interested in gossip or slander, but the secular courts are, and this is a blessing. Thank God for the state, and the laws on libel and slander, for if you are personally slandered at church, then you have every right to uphold the law and sue those who commit crimes. Peter in his first letter, admonishes his readers and says that if you are stupid enough to incur the wrath of the law because you participate in crime, then you have only yourself to blame (1 Peter 2:20). He also fully expects that those who seek to follow Jesus will suffer slander and abuse from within the church and outside (1 Peter 3: 15-16).

If you go to churches now, you are in the thick of the Culture War. It will not be long before someone says something slanderous against someone or even against you. If you follow Jesus, they will hate you, if you do not support their fascism, their fraud, or their corrupt behavior, they will come after you. Churches today are cesspools of this form of immorality. This behavior is intolerable, and it is illegal. If you and your life are personally brought into question by a priest from the pulpit, – for example, if they call out your name and call you personally immoral- then you can sue them for slander, and you probably should.

About Covid Hysteria, I can say this. What happened was vile and criminal. At the same time, so many people said vile things about *'unvaccinated'* people. They said for example that *'unvaccinated people are criminals and domestic terrorists.'* They said that *'unvaccinated people are all fascists.'* They said, *'unvaccinated people are illiterate, uneducated, and stupid.'* This was not the Culture War. This was propaganda, state-led abuse of the population. This was state-sponsored slander and state-sponsored abuse. Many churches went along with it, apparently to *'keep people safe,'* but in Australia, many were happy to take government subsidies as well. The churches should still be closed because Covid is killing more people each day than it did at the height of the *'pandemic.'* Open churches today are part of a national culture supportive of the spread of a contagious disease.

The churches have however moved on. The focus now is the Culture War and in Anglo-Saxon cultures, it is the war on gay and transgender people, especially kids, it is the war on same-sex marriage, and the war on abortion. The Culture War has nothing whatsoever to do with the gospel of Jesus Christ. I urge you to have nothing to do with it. Do not participate, do not get involved, and say nothing, or you will end up saying something you will regret. It is awful to read the vile abusive comments between Christians engaged in whatever latest political issue occupies their attention.

This Culture War is not Christianity, and it is a perverse re-run of Prohibition and its variants in the West that corrupted the church from the end of the nineteenth century till the Depression. In those days, alcohol was a great sin, like sex is today, and Christians put temperance alongside conversion. If you came to Christ, you needed to stop drinking alcohol. It was insisted upon everywhere. If you converted to Christ, then you needed to sign the pledge. These days, to become a Christian in many places, you need to sign a statement that you agree with the traditional definition of marriage or gender. The advocates of Prohibition promoted a moralism that was not Christianity and had nothing to do with the gospel. Those who promote this *'marriage-based'* gospel or gendered faith are the same, they are not Christians, they are fascists, and they do not promote the gospel.

Like James, I stumble all the time, and I am not perfect. The cross of Jesus Christ reminds me of my constant need for his grace. Why add more fuel to the fire of your belly and jump on the bandwagon of the Culture War? Is it not better to guard your tongue, mind your language, and even offer kindness and love to your enemies? If you are a follower of Jesus Christ, do you have any enemies? James reminds us that there is no such thing as free speech. Jesus also warns us that *'anyone who says, 'You fool!' will be in danger of the fire of hell' (Matthew 5: 22).*

There, but for the grace of God, go I.

What can you say to God?

I have said so far that there is no such thing as free speech. I hold to that statement as being true. For the citizen, there are many restraints on what can be said, and these days, quite legitimate boundaries exist to protect people from *'free speech.'* We also discovered that speech is never free; there are always consequences to what we say to others. The New Testament roundly condemns gossip and slander, which, once again, are restraints on the right of *'free speech.'* Slander gets 24 mentions in the New Testament, while gossip gets 2. Even so, this is more than *'sexual immorality'* at 22 mentions. Does your local church pay as much attention to slander as it does sexual immorality? Probably not. The fact is that what we say can wreak havoc more than pretty much anything. We like to think in the West that we live in a world of peace, but our words cut and kill, wound, and maim and we go about our lives with gossip and slander coursing through our veins more often than the Covid booster shots. The interesting question is of course, why Christian Fascists never talk about the sin of slander or gossip. Without gossip and slander, many Christians would have no reason to attend Sunday services. Slander and gossip are the lifeblood of the church.

While free speech does not exist, how about our relationship with God? What can you say to God? Now here, this is where it gets interesting, very interesting. From the first book of the Bible, Genesis, to the last book, Revelation, the answer is simple: you can say anything to God. God is God. This means he can handle the questions, the accusations, the frustrations, and the fears. God is there to hear our prayers, and that goes for those who know God and those who do not. Otherwise, how could people who know God ever know God if he only hears the ones he already knows? Prayer is not only for those who do not know God but also for those who have known him their whole lives. We need to be careful what we say to each other, but we can say anything to God.

Christian Fascists do not agree. How are we not surprised? They have religion to prop up their material interests. The last thing they want is people who pray and believe in prayer. They will say things like *'prayer only changes the one praying.'* The old Christian Fascists (back in the day) used to talk about *'God's will.'* They supported slavery in America for example. Their view was that it was *'God's will'* and we had no right to question *'God's will.'*

Twisted or appropriated versions of Calvinistic predestination were used to justify the idea that God had ordained some (white people) to freedom and some (African Americans) to slavery. It was not our place to question or protest to God what he has ordained. The British did the same with their vile and Satanic class system. Yes, it is Satanic. It is evil. The *'upstairs downstairs'* society was sick and twisted. Everyone had their place, and it was ordained by God, and no one had the right to question what he had created. But

God did not create slavery, men did, and God did not approve of the British class system either.

The place we should go to investigate this further is the Psalms, written many hundreds of years before the arrival of Jesus the Messiah. Many Psalms are attributed to King David. They were put together as a compilation of songs that may have been used during worship at the Temple in Jerusalem. The Psalms are the place to go if we are interested in knowing how people spoke to God in the past. It is surprising to know that even though the Psalmists wrote well over 2,000 years ago, their Psalms read as if they were written yesterday. They often speak to the natural fears of the human experience, and they plumb the heights of joy to the depths of despair. It is also interesting to note that these were probably songs to use for liturgical purposes, that is Psalms used during Temple worship. We know from the books of Ezra and Nehemiah that after the return from Exile, there were schools of musicians who played in the Temple and in worship. They, no doubt used some of the Psalms recorded in that book.

It is also interesting to note their use of music because the Psalms are often raw, painful, revelatory statements of the frailty of human life. Hardly the kind of songs you would expect in a church. It is perhaps one reason why the Psalms are often ignored these days or only the *'nice'* ones get a mention. Some of the Psalms are beautiful, some are tragic, and some are dark. Take Psalm 6 for example. The Psalmist is in trouble and yet he/she does not hesitate to verbalize their pain to God. They know God listens. They also make sure he knows exactly what is going on. For example, some excerpts: *'I am faint, 'my bones are in agony. My soul is in deep anguish. How long, Lord, how long?'* The Psalmist also says: *'I am worn out from my groaning. All night long I flood my bed with weeping and drench my couch with tears. My eyes grow weak with sorrow.'*

What can we say to God? The Psalmist suggests anything and everything. It is not the presence of evil or sadness or trouble or strife that strikes me. The Psalmist seems to accept the reality of life. How much better off we might be if we had this attitude. We in the West, never seem to be happy, but the Psalmist's lament is couched in the phrase, *'how long?'* How long? How long will this pain continue? It is going on, it is continuing. When will it end? It is in the depths of personal despair that the Psalmist is deeply honest with

God not about what is happening, but how what is happening affects him and his relationship with God. The suffering of the Psalmist takes them to God in prayer, not in the abuse of others, or ranting and raving, or protesting, or going to war, but their response is to take it to God.

Like Psalm 6, Psalm 80 is explicitly set to music or liturgical accompaniment. Once again, it is not a song that one would expect to hear in a church today. The Psalmist takes God on, his decisions, his actions, and his covenant with Israel. These are fighting words. The Psalmist intercedes for the people to God, and he complains to God about what is happening in his life. He says in verses 4-6:

'How long, Lord God Almighty, will your anger smolder against the prayers of your people? You have fed them with the bread of tears; you have made them drink tears by the bowlful; you have made us an object of derision to our neighbors, and our enemies mock us.'

This prayer is angry, it is tearful, it is honest. He repeats three times his desire that God would restore them, implying that they have fallen from a great height and are suffering. He says simply: *'make your face shine on us, that we may be saved.'* This is not what the Christians today in the West would say. He or she assumes naturally that God always shines his face towards us, that everything in the garden is rosy, and that a relationship with God is the path to the good life, but not here. This is a realistic prayer of a man aware of who he is, and what is happening around him, conscious of the judgment of God upon his nation. How long with your anger smolder against us? Once again, God will never be angry with us, say Western Christians, because God blesses our nation, doesn't he? Check the Bible. He doesn't. He blesses people not nations.

Psalm 55 was used in liturgy, which is fascinating for it is a prayer of a person who wanted to escape the current situation but cannot, and in facing it, must endure intense unhappiness. For example, read the words that are used in verses 4 and 5: *'My heart is in anguish within me. The terrors of death have fallen on me. Fear and trembling have beset me; horror has overwhelmed me.'* This is not a prayer for ordinary things. The Psalmist is in the pit of despair, in the throngs of terrible fear and a nightmare scenario. It is betrayal, the pain caused by the closest of companions, it is what they have done, and continue to do. He writes in verses 12 to 14:

'If an enemy were insulting me, I could endure it; if a foe were rising against me, I could hide. But it is you, a man like myself, my companion, my close friend, with whom I once enjoyed sweet fellowship at the house of God, as we walked about among the worshipers.'

This fear is personal. Curiously he says that he could handle battle, and face-to-face combat with his enemy, and that is not a problem. His problem is that his friend is now a traitor and is bringing him down as he knows his weaknesses and vulnerabilities.

The more you pray to God, the more you understand yourself and God, and the more you understand how God works in his world and in our lives. God acts and God speaks. God changes. He builds and he destroys, and he listens to us. What can you say to God? Anything you want. He is God. He can handle it.

Faith gives us freedom of speech

It is only faith that gives us freedom of speech. Before faith, we were not free. We were oppressed. We did not understand. Sorrows were endless. The pain was unquenched. Minds were darkened. Faith, God's greatest gift to us, enabled us to see him clearly and see us honestly, to need him fully.

These days we love to talk. We are not known as quiet people, meditative people, or reflective people. Instead, we are known as people who talk, a lot, and loudly. We fill our lives with words, and we think that if we stop speaking, we will die suddenly and then all the things we want to say will be left unsaid. Most people in the West have likely said everything important that they ever needed to say on one Saturday morning at the local café, and that was three weeks ago!

There are two types of words, words that fall to the ground and words that do not. These are words that we forget and words we remember. Most of what we say is forgotten and it disappears. It is gone. A good society respects the words of the people. A sensible society responds genuinely to the will of the people. I am not speaking of democracy here. We do not need to embrace the European or American model of democracy to have a society where the will of the people is respected. All societies need to respond to the people to some degree or there will be a violent revolution. History shows that societies that ignore the people will perish.

It is certainly true that the Western political class has no interest in what you have to say. They are sitting pretty, laughing all the way to the bank, fully expecting that no one will ever topple them. Your words do not matter, and since all the parties are the same in the West, nothing will change. Your words will fall to the ground.

People in power do not care about you, your lives, or your situation. They are silent, dismissive, callous, and indifferent. I have said before and I will say again, this attitude is a sign of national decline. The West is falling, and the rich have their heads deep in the trough and they simply don't care about you, if they ever did.

If there ever was a time for our words to matter, it would be now. It is not that our words matter in the sense that we are saying anything profound or earth-shattering, but they are our words, and they are important to us. We speak because what we speak about matters to us, and there is one word often on our lips and in our hearts.

This word has to do with fear. We are fearful, we are afraid, we despair, and we ache for so many things that we once had or we long for or that have been elusive. These words matter, because they come from within our hearts, they stir in the belly, they churn in our stomach and our gut and we speak to them with earnestness, genuine spirit, honesty, and plainness.

There is only one who makes sure our words do not fall to the ground. Indeed, there is only one who takes our words, our accents, our intonations, our grammar, our stuttering, our frail expressions, and our incomplete ideas and holds them in his hand. He remembers them, he cherishes them, he hears them, and he does not forget.

That person is God. There is only one freedom of speech that is eternal, and that is from faith. There is only one person qualified to hear our words and hold them and keep them in his heart and that is God.

Unlike the government or the church, God is not deaf. In a world of fear, anxiety, and despair, forget the government, they are not listening, forget the President, he doesn't care, forget the church, they are too busy trying to get to your pockets and your money. It is to God we ought to direct our thoughts, prayers, requests, and complaints, not the government. We know that government will fail us, lie to us, and betray us, but not God.

Those who follow Jesus and walk with God have no reason to place all their confidence in society or democracy because the heart and soul of life is our relationship with God. True freedom of speech has to do with us speaking to God freely and we can do that because of the Lord Jesus Christ.

It is faith that gives us freedom of speech. This is in the Bible, surprisingly enough. This is found in Paul's letter to Ephesians chapter 3 and verse 13. It reads:

'In him and through faith in him we may approach God with freedom and confidence' (Ephesians 3: 13).

This is only one verse, and it is tucked into a broader discussion of the role of the assembly as the exhibition or display to the world of the wisdom of God, a kind of proclamation to the rulers and authorities of society, spiritual and temporal. The assembly of Christians is to be different. It is not of course in the West. It is simply a mirror of the state and when it speaks, it does only in the areas approved by the government.

Early Christians were different. They got noticed. Whenever Christians follow Christ, they also get attention. John Hus, William Tyndale, Cranmer, the Oxford martyrs, so many of them over the years, they all got noticed for following Jesus and the church-state killed them.

The ones who follow Jesus get persecuted, often by the church. Jesus said so. He said, if you follow me, you will be persecuted. If the church is not persecuted in the West, then it means it is not following Christ. It is that simple. If you are in a local Christian assembly and you want to follow Jesus, they will oppose you, the enemies of Christ, in that assembly, they always do. Assemblies that have no conflict are going straight to Hell because they are already dead. There are a lot of dead churches.

Leaving aside the potential of the assembly to be a light to the world and the conflict within, we come to what Paul says about free speech. It is an enigmatic verse and says more than it appears to at first glance. Many verses of the New Testament are the same. They require careful reading, not casual glances. This verse is no different.

Paul writes *'In him and through faith in him we may approach God with freedom and confidence' (Ephesians 3: 12-13).* Paul is saying that in Jesus, and through faith in Christ, we can approach God in prayer and come into his presence with freedom and confidence.

In other words, without fear, without trembling, and without reservation. We do not sulk in the back or get in the back door, nor are we ushered to the servant's church or the back streets for the ungodly, but we enter his presence in confidence and freedom.

Faith enables us to stand before God. This is not the only time this idea is mentioned in the New Testament. In Romans 5: 2, Paul says: *'through whom we have gained access by faith into this grace in which we stand. And we rejoice in the hope of the glory of God.'* In 2 Corinthians 3: 4, Paul reminds us that *'Such confidence before God is ours through Christ.'* In Ephesians 2: 18, Paul says *'For through Him we both have access to the Father by one Spirit.'*

The author of Hebrews (4:16) also says *'Let us then approach the throne of grace with confidence, so that we may receive mercy and find grace to help us in our time of need.'* Indeed, Paul also said in Philippians 4: 6: *'Do not be anxious about anything, but in every situation, by prayer and petition, with thanksgiving, present your requests to God.'*

Faith gives us freedom of speech before God. It is no wonder the church hates Paul. Imagine, people praying to God and avoiding the need for their priests, and the illusion of the Mass, or the confessional. Imagine, Christians boldly going up to God in confidence and speaking to him as if he knows them and welcomes them.

They are not welcome at church, you must be silent there, or speak when you are spoken to, seen, and not heard right, that's their attitude. Only it is not God's attitude. You are free, you are free to enter his presence and you are free to speak. Thank God!

What does freedom of speech mean to God?

While we are to be careful what we say to others made in the image of God, we can say whatever we want to God when we speak to him as he can handle our words. We need not couch our terms or mind our manners or mince our words when speaking to God. It is remarkable because it is counterintuitive. One would expect that the God of the universe, who created all things would be more demanding, more restrictive, and more like us, and that is the point. Even when the Word became flesh and dwelt among us, Jesus at his worst was better than the best of us, and at his best, he was truly human in a way that none of us could ever be, though we have all sought to be at some point.

Indeed, the freedom to speak to God is the truest in the world. It is the only truly free words we ever speak. God is not silent, nor does he expect us to sit in silence. God expects people to speak to him, and he expects his children to speak to him boldly and confidently. The problem today is not simply that people do not pray or speak to God, but that their prayers are presented to a God they neither know nor understand. This is a problem because we whisper when we should shout, we cower when we should assert, and we qualify when we should expect. For some reason, we think that we should be very careful in how we speak to God and what words to use.

This is strange because the way we can speak to God has never changed. From Adam who talked with God in the cool of the day to Enoch who walked with God, to Abraham whom God considered a friend, to Moses who met God in the burning bush, to Elijah who met God at Horeb, to name but a few encounters, they all have one thing in common and that is that God speaks to us in words we can understand so that he can have a conversation. If your church does not allow a conversation or expects you to *'sit down, shut up, and do as you are told,'* then you only have yourself to blame, for whenever Christians gather, they converse with God, they commune with God, and they worship a God who listens, speaks, and acts. Those silent churches, that expect silence and awe and obedience are not places where God dwells, for God is constantly speaking, even in the silence.

In the past, the author of the Hebrews puts it, *'In the past, God spoke to our ancestors through the prophets at many times and in various ways, but in these last days he has spoken to us by his Son'* (Hebrews 1:1-2). What he is trying to get across in this letter is something quite profound and is completely lost in the church which seems to think that being in the church gives people the license to speak for God words he has never spoken. This is perhaps one of the legacies of American Christianity. Maybe you have been to one of these churches where the pastor gets up and pretends to be speaking the words of the Holy Spirit. He is not. He is making it up. It is vanity, it is pride. God speaks through his word, the Bible. When those ministers of the gospel have so exhausted the text of scripture and so drenched their people in the truths of experience lived out in the text, then sure knock yourselves out with *'words from the Lord,'* but if you have ever read the gospels or even the words of Jesus, then you know that these men who claim to speak for God are not speaking from God at all.

While the way God speaks to us has changed, the way we are to speak to God has not. The examples throughout the Bible, from Abraham in bargaining with God over the fate of Sodom, to Israel wrestling with God until daybreak, to Moses complaining about his speech impediments, to Paul's prayers of joy whilst in prison, are all reminders that those who know God can talk to him and hold nothing back.

God wants us to tell him what is on our minds. God says to us: *'what do you want to say?'* and we never say it. He says *'Ok, let's hear it,'* and we don't tell him anything. God says: *'tell me what's on your mind'* and we give him dead liturgy, rote prayers, and babble. What does freedom of speech mean to God? Simply being honest with him. Our prayers are a product of our position and this is not our position in society, it is not up or down or left or right, or rich or poor. Our position is our position in relation to God, the only position that matters. This position is one of grace and mercy. This position is one of security and assurance and this position is one we did not carve out for ourselves.

It was God who enabled us to be in this position. It was God who provided the place and the possibility for us to stand before him, and it was God who is the position. We do not enter the presence of God through the church, or through the priest, or through the Mass, or through baptism, or through penance or through confession, but simply because of Him, that is Christ.

Throughout Paul's letter to the Ephesians, there is the recurring phrase *'in him,'* which means *'in Christ.'* There are over ten times where the phrase 'in Him' is mentioned in the first part of Chapter 1 of Ephesians. It is through our personal relationship with the risen Savior Jesus, the Messiah, that we are restored to fellowship with God. This means it is not our relationship with the church, our church membership, or church attendance. It is this relationship with Christ. This is the heart of it. This is the essence of it. We have every spiritual blessing *'in Christ,'* God chose us *'in him,'* God's purposes for us were fulfilled *'in him,'* so that all things in the world come together in Christ, *'in him'* we were chosen, *'in him'* we put our hope, *'in him'* we were included, the Holy Spirit was given to us *'in him.'*

Note what Paul is not saying. He is not saying that we find any of these blessings in the church or at the feet of our priest, or at baptism, or in the Mass, or in the liturgy, or in obedience, or in ritual or regulations, but they are all to be found only and exclusively in Christ, for without him we have nothing but with him we have everything.

Christ is the only way we can know God. Our position in relationship to God only exists because of Christ. It is only possible because of Christ. Indeed, it is not about baptism or church, family, or creed. Our faith is about our position before God and indeed our position within God, for Christ is God and the Father is God, and the Holy Spirit is God. We are not excluded from God, and we are not outside of God, and we do not need to wait till Sunday until we meet God, we are *'in him'* and in Christ, and we have been sealed by the Holy Spirit who is our deposit guaranteeing our inheritance.

If we are in Christ, then it assumes there was a time when we were not in Christ. Paul wrote: *'And you also were included in Christ when you heard the message of truth, the gospel of your salvation. When you believed, you were marked in him with a seal, the promised Holy Spirit' (Ephesians 1: 13).*

This is exactly what John says in his Gospel: all you need do is believe in the Son, and you shall have eternal life. Now, many Christian people labor the idea of repentance, the idea that before you come to God before you can have faith, you need to repent and give up your sins and turn from your wicked ways before you are qualified to have faith. Christian Fascists tell you that you can baptize a child who has no words to speak or no choices to make except to defecate, dribble, and dote and that without this child's consent or permission, they are forced into the kingdom of God. This should have been the warning to all of you of the horrors of the church, of the nightmare of organized religion. Even at birth, you had no choice, and this was the template for a life of servitude in a world of Christian Fascism. Contrast this with the words of Paul: *'when you heard the message of truth,'* when you chose to listen, when you lifted your ears to hear, when you turned your face to your father or your friend or your lover and heard the words of Jesus speaking to you, and you believed. Paul says: *'And you also were included in Christ when you heard the message of truth, the gospel of your salvation. When you believed.'*

Now, included in this hearing and believing is a turning to God because you need to turn to God to have faith in him, but there is no need to provide proof of repentance for faith. Faith is simply faith. It is trust in God and his promises. The Christian people always telling you to repent are those who do not understand faith, and probably don't have any and they will be the kind of people who have a moral righteousness that depends on them and not on Christ.

Paul goes further and says that *'through faith in him'* we may enter God's presence with boldness and confidence. This faith is critical. In Greek, it means faith, belief, or trust. John uses the term believe while Paul uses the term faith, but they are both essentially the same. They refer to a sense of trust, but trust in what? A simple trust in who Jesus is, who sent him, and what he did for us.

Faith is turning history into testimony. It is this simple understanding that goes beyond a mere assent of intellectual acceptance of the morality of God and the necessity of grace, but an actual submission to the truth of this for me or you, a genuine internalization of this reality. This *'faith in him'* transforms our life. Simply believing facts about him changes nothing. Paul is not talking about intellectual mind games but a changed heart, a new beginning, and a new relationship with God.

This is where it gets interesting. Paul made the statement that *'in him and through faith in him'* and we understand that. We reach this place together. Many Christians would go this far. Yes, they would say, I agree, but they would stop here. The next few words are not for them, they are not priests or ministers, and they do not have a seminary degree, nor are they white or European. These are some of the excuses people have made over the years. Many Christians do not believe the next phrase belongs to them. They would say *'they can'*, not *'we can.'* This is the evil of clericalism, the evil of Christian Fascism.

The controversial phrase is the following: *'we may.'* It is the first-person plural. It is the plural, there is no mistaking it. And who are the *'we'*? Well, all people included in the previous clause, are those who are in Christ and have faith in him. It is a verb, a word of action, *'we may.'* It is all-inclusive. This includes you; this includes all who come to faith, with no exceptions. The priest has no hotline to God. None. You do not need to confess to him. He is no better than you. Never was, never will be. What does freedom of speech mean to God? It means we all may enter his presence. God has no favorites. *'We may'* is for all. There is no hierarchy in the assembly of God.

What Paul is saying is that we may all enter God's presence with boldness and confidence. This entering of God's presence could also be seen as an admission or access or approach. The words all convey the same thing – there is no obstacle, and there is nothing stopping you from entering God's presence, indeed, you have by virtue of your position in Christ. You are continually in the presence of God. But Paul doesn't just talk about access, he is speaking of two words to qualify how we might enter the presence of God. They are *'boldness'* and *'confidence.'* The Greek word for boldness is fascinating. It has an interesting meaning, and I don't know why this is clouded in the translations. It speaks to the idea of outspokenness, being blunt and frank, and this is the idea of speaking freely to God, without needing to be polite.

This is what speaking boldly means. If you have a problem with this and you cannot speak to God unless you couch your prayers in long respectful language, then you have a problem with God and a problem with God's word. Out with it, says God, tell me what is on your mind. So, we can be frank with God, honest, up-front, no holds barred. He is God, he can handle it. We also have confidence, which means trust. We can trust that what we say to God he hears because we are in his presence, and we are in Christ. What is free speech before God? It is free, unrestrained, emotive, genuine, and honest. The rest is fake. Save your polite platitudes and beautiful poetry for church. In your prayers, open your heart to God. Some Christians get hung up with whether we can call God *'Daddy'* or Father in the Lord's Prayer, that is not the point. This is semantic. The way we talk to God is free. The entire way of communicating with God is free. What does freedom of speech mean to God? It means we can speak freely to the one in whose presence we can enter because of the faith we have in His Son. That is free speech.

When does God want to hear from you?

Have you ever been tired? Exhausted? Weary? In our lives, we have a lot of restlessness. I do not know your situation. Maybe you experience a lot of restlessness and frustration in life. For me, the last two years, from early 2020 until a new months ago, have been two years of weariness. We were told this was the most severe disease in our lifetime and we needed to stop the spread of Covid. Two years of sustained lies from people in power over lockdowns and mandates and passports, now ending with admissions that Covid is only the flu and no harm done. More people are dying from Covid in November 2022 than at the height of the martial law madness in 2021. The media who supported Covid Zero policies last year are now condemning China this year for Beijing's support of Covid Zero policies. They are arguing the Chinese should be free, a gross hypocrisy of course because they want to give Chinese people what they so devoutly denied Australians for two years.

For many Australians, it was their first taste in the deceit of democracy. I am, like many, a student of international relations and this was not my first exposure. Twenty years of deceit over the War on Terror, for example, perpetual corruption and financial mismanagement of the economy my entire adult life, and a political world where the best and brightest are ousted by the mediocre and forgettable by the faction bosses and their backers in industry. In Covid, two years where our lives were placed on hold, for nothing. It was all a hideous lie. It was all a fraud. No one will take responsibility. No one will be punished. Welcome to democracy. See yourselves out.

But Covid was not the only time for weariness or the only source for weariness. People in Yemen have been at war for years, and people in Ethiopia have as well. No one cares, least of all the West.

After all, they are Africans and Arabs, and their lives are not as important as Ukrainians and Westerners. We have discovered during the civil war in Ukraine, that the life of a European is worth more than the life of an African or Arab or anyone. So much for political correctness.

Thank God that the Ukrainians are white people because if they were not, no one would know what was going on there at all. If you don't agree, tell me who is to blame in the current Sri Lanka mess, the civil war in Ethiopia, or the war in Yemen? And where is all the money for the Middle East that we left in ruins in a series of wars that were completely amoral and godless?

We don't live in unusual times, nor even remarkable times. This is not the greatest time in history. We may be living at a turning point, but few of us will be involved with that. Life is simply life. It is ordinary. The people in the past didn't know about the future because they lived in the past, but they faced the problems that we face, and the people before that. It is amazing when you read the Bible because it is like reading what happened yesterday, not 2,000 years ago.

It is perhaps why the author of the Hebrews says this about the Bible in Hebrews 4: 12-13:

'For the word of God is alive and active. Sharper than any double-edged sword, it penetrates even to dividing soul and spirit, joints, and marrow; it judges the thoughts and attitudes of the heart. Nothing in all creation is hidden from God's sight. Everything is uncovered and laid bare before the eyes of him to whom we must give account.'

God seeks to uncover our inner workings. When does God want to hear from you? He wants to search our hearts. The Bible speaks to us because it speaks to our hearts, our thoughts, and our inner being. It divides, that is, it separates, clarifies, and sorts. The Bible goes beyond our actions, words, and public life, and goes to our hearts, the places we keep silent, doors we keep closed, and memories we keep hidden.

God uncovers all of them, not for public viewing, but for his own, because it is before God all must give an account of their lives. God is the one who knows us, can see us, and can perceive us, regardless of the barriers we erect for others. They say the heart is our hidden life, but not for God. He sees all. He is especially interested in the thoughts and attitudes of the heart. What secrets he must see, what truths he must discern, what wonders he must experience, in the hidden life of the human heart.

The question we must ask ourselves is: why is God searching our hearts? What is he looking for? These words are very popular among Christians as they speak about the authority and the power and the presence of the word of God. Yet, their inclusion at all in the letter to the Hebrews is not immediately obvious to the reader. Put simply, the writer of the Hebrews is saying that resting or abiding in God is often at risk due to the hardness of our hearts and the word of God is the way that God discerns our faithfulness to him.

The entire book of Hebrews is about finding this rest in God through Jesus Christ. His canvass is not simply the beginning of the little apostolic community in Jerusalem after the ascension of Christ. His canvas considers the whole scope of God's dealings with Israel from Abraham right up to the advent of Christ. Hebrews is a remarkable book. He is perhaps the only writer in the New Testament who truly grasps the depth, width, and height of God's love for his people as well as the identity and consequences of the person of Jesus Christ.

In chapter 3, we are told to *'fix your thoughts on Jesus, whom we acknowledge as our apostle and high priest'* (Hebrews 3:1). Jesus has been faithful in his role of the Son over *'God's house. And we are his house if indeed we hold firmly to our confidence and the hope in which we glory'* (Hebrews 3: 6). This is not a house made with bricks or mortar, but it is the people of God. A key idea in Hebrews 3 is that of perseverance, moving forward, keeping one's heart in check, not resting on past achievements, living in the present, and going on. The author quotes Psalm 95 where God told his people that he was angry with them and that they would not be able to enter his rest, which was the Promised Land of Israel.

The warning for us who believe in Christ is simple:

'See to it, brothers, that none of you has a sinful, unbelieving heart that turns away from the living God. But encourage one another daily, as long as it is called "Today," so that none of you may be hardened by sin's deceitfulness. We have come to share in

Christ if indeed we hold our original conviction firmly to the very end' (Hebrews 3: 12-14).

The Word of God is the antidote to a hardening heart. It is not the church, it is not liturgy, it is not your Creed, or your statement of faith, or the principles of your party, or sect, but it is the word of God. For the author of the Hebrews, the problem of faith is the hardness of heart, or rather that the authenticity of faith is tested by the hardness of heart to the Holy Spirit and the word of God through life. This hardness of heart is indicative of unbelief and the way to discourage this is to encourage one another daily if it is called Today. When does God want to hear from you? Faith in God is a daily faith, one step at a time.

We need to encourage one another daily. He does not say, *'go to church and you will get your weekly Mass/Sermon from God,'* but he says, *'encourage one another daily.'* He is not speaking about your pastor, he is talking about you – you are to encourage each other daily. Many Christian Fascists hate Hebrews for this reason. It is too revolutionary. It does away with the need for *'church'* entirely, making faith a daily reality, not a Sunday ritual. Did not our Lord say, *'give us this day our daily bread'*?

In Chapter 4, the author of the Hebrews goes on to say *'Therefore, since the promise of entering his rest still stands, let us be careful that none of you be found to have fallen short of it' (Hebrews 4:1).* The Sabbath Day, which has become an idol to many Christians is therefore just an image of the day of rest to come, the Sabbath Rest of God, which is Christ. Of course, for Jews, the Sabbath is Saturday. Christians changed it to Sunday, but Hebrews points out that the more important reality is not the day change but the possibility of true rest in God found in the Lord Jesus Christ and eternal life with God.

He says *'There remains, then, a Sabbath-rest for the people of God; for anyone who enters God's rest also rests from their works, just as God did from his. Let us, therefore, make every effort to enter that rest, so that no one will perish by following their example of disobedience' (Hebrews 4: 9-11).* There are parallels with John's idea of abiding or remaining in Christ in his Gospel (see John 15). The Sabbath Rest is essentially the rest that comes from knowing God and finding peace in him. This rest is daily, it is continual, it doesn't stay one day of the week, but becomes every day.

It is immediately after these verses that we have the famous verses about the word of God being living and active. Therefore, the context implies that the Sabbath Rest is the goal, the word of God is essential for discouraging the hardness of heart that comes as proof of disqualification. God's work in searching for us helps to prove our authenticity of faith. He is not speaking about a process of elimination, but rather, a living and active faith that does not rest on the past or past achievements but one that exists Today, not yesterday, one that is living and breathing and moving forward. God's word is not for yesterday, but for today. God wants us to walk with him, not stand still. He wants us to keep moving forward, not looking back. Is there ever a time when God wants to hear from us? Yes, of course, he wants to hear from us every day, because he is a God who walks with us, in our life, and never leaves us.

Why can we pray to God?

Why can we pray to God? It may seem like a strange question, but it is an important one. I don't know about you, but life is tough. Life can be mean, it can be cruel, it can be hard, and unforgiving. I don't know where you are today. Maybe it is a good day for you or a bad day. In the Hebrew Bible, there were many images used by the people who compiled the Old Testament to describe a place where we could escape from the toughness of life and enjoy peace with God. There are a few I like.

The Psalmists often talk about God as being a shield. We do not go to battle these days, we have the military for that, and they seem to be constantly at war these days for one reason or another. But in ancient times, the shield was essential to use in a fight, as both a defensive and offensive weapon.

Another term or idea that the Psalmists used was that of a refuge. Psalm 46 speaks of God being our strength and refuge. In Israel, there were cities of refuge where people could flee if they had accidentally killed someone. These were places where they could escape, until the matter came before the courts.

Then there was the Temple. The Temple, I hear you say? You don't like temples, do you? Well, I don't like fake temples such as the churches which are the modern high places, but the Temple of Jerusalem was where God met with his people Israel. The Hebrew Bible taught that God wanted his people to gather where he was, for fellowship, reconciliation, and prayer. One of the Psalms that speak to me about this connection with Jerusalem is Psalm 84: *'How lovely is your dwelling place, Lord Almighty! My soul yearns, even faints, for the courts of the Lord,'* or *'Better is one day in your courts than a thousand elsewhere; I would rather be a doorkeeper in the house of my God than dwell in the tents of the wicked.'* The Psalmist is not speaking of a place, but the place where God meets with his people. This is to dwell with God, to pray to him, to enjoy fellowship with him, to read his word and meditate upon him, living out the life he expects of us.

The New Testament is different of course. There is no building where God dwells, no church structure he inhabits. He is with his people, drawn from every nation, including Russia and in God's family, God sees Americans and Russians as the same – he has no favorites. For the Christian, it is Christ who unites us by faith. It is the person of Christ who makes salvation possible. Jesus is the Great High Priest; he is the one who gives us confidence because of his faithfulness to God. He was faithful when we could not be, he lived a life we could not, and died and rose again.

It is in the miracle of the incarnation that God lived among us and knew our lives and experiences. He knew weariness, fear, terror, sadness, and hardship. Christ was fully human, and he experienced it all, all the gamut of human life. God knows it is tough because he has experienced it as well. He knows about it. He walked those streets.

Why can we pray to God? Because Jesus understands. The only way we can experience rest in our lives is if we speak to someone who can help us. The Christian goes to God when only God can help. If it is the doctor, then we should go to the clinic, if it is parents or spouse then it makes sense there as well. We cannot rest until we go to God and tell him everything.

But how do we know he will even listen? He is in heaven, and up there, and how could he understand us and our lives? Many Christians believe God is only in heaven and that he does not exist in our hearts and minds, and they have such a low view of the Spirit of God that they think the only way he speaks is through babble and nonsense. But you have God's word, and you can read it, right, so yes, that is how the Holy Spirit speaks to us.

Why can we pray to God? Because Jesus died for our sins. But we can go to God in confidence in our prayers and in our demands and requests because there is someone in heaven who has been here and has lived our lives and experienced our pain. He died for our sins, in our place, on the cross, enabling us to have faith in God. Through his death, Jesus connects us to the Father, to a right relationship with him.

That is the Lord Jesus Christ, who can understand us and our prayers. Hebrews 4: 15-16 says these words:

'For we do not have a high priest who is unable to empathize with our weaknesses, but we have one who has been tempted in every way, just as we are—yet he did not sin. Let us then approach God's throne of grace with confidence, so that we may receive mercy and find grace to help us in our time of need.'

We can approach God because of Christ, because of his work for us on the cross. We can approach God and ask in confidence because his throne is not the throne of judgment and condemnation – no, that is the throne in your local church – the throne in heaven is the throne of grace.

Why can we pray to God? Because of God's language, and grace. Grace is God's language and the method of delivery to us was the blood of Christ, the only one who could be both man and God, able to intercede for us to the Father and able to live our lives as our brother, the only one who could. His entry into the presence of God enables us to enter the presence of God, not through the Mass, not through confession, not through the priest, but simply and straight away into the actual presence of God, every day and always, in his presence for he is the God of mercy and the God of grace.

You don't need to go to church to pray, you can pray anywhere, anytime. It is to God we can pray, and he is the God who acts and responds in love to his people, even in times of silence when he speaks the loudest. You don't need to go to church to pray to God or even believe in Christ.

Jesus prayed everywhere, and so can we, because the Father of Jesus was his Father everywhere and he is ours as well. He is not our Father only on Sundays, but every day and his language is grace and mercy to all in need.

4   CAN AMERICA CALM OUR FEARS?

Does political power bring freedom from fear?

In February 2022, the civil war in Ukraine that began in 2014 escalated when Russia decided to intervene to protect several pro-Russian provinces in the East. America suddenly decided that war was evil and illegal, and declared a state of war with Russia under the *'Stand with Ukraine'* slogan, thus beginning World War 3 or at the very least a new Cold War with distinct flavors and echoes of the Korean and Vietnam conflicts. America's allies followed suit and now everyone seems to believe the principle that nations are not allowed to invade other nations, and those that do must pay reparations, as well as be accountable for war crimes such as the imprisonment of journalists. This excludes Julian Assange of course, and the West assumes that any accusation of war crimes against their troops in any theatre of war can be dismissed as fake news and Russian disinformation. Indeed, this new American principle of international relations, the New Peace doctrine, is that all that America does abroad is righteous and must be accepted without question, and all that Russia and China do abroad is evil and monstrous and must be condemned without reservation.

America's discovery of global peace – the New Peace - and the eternal renunciation of war came less than a year after the last American troops withdrew from Afghanistan (August 30, 2021), following America's illegal and immoral invasion of that sovereign nation twenty years before. America also invaded and destroyed Iraq, Libya, and Syria, and in the process of this conflict, hundreds of thousands of civilians perished. There will be no tribunals to investigate these deaths, no punishments for war crimes, and no regrets. Many in the American ruling class are still upset by the withdrawal and can say that the American invasion of Afghanistan was justified, while the Russian invasion of Ukraine was evil with a straight face. That the global media says nothing says everything. The global media corporations wipe their mouths and say, *'we have done nothing wrong,'* while whipping up hatred against all Russian people around the world, even little children at school who are bullied because of their nationality.

During the War on Terror against the Taliban, ISIS, and friends, the American state was careful to distinguish between combatants and culture, though they did this very poorly, and there was much confusion. In this civil war between the American puppet regime in Kyiv, Western 'advisers,' with Western weapons, and the pro-Russian provinces in the east, the West has decided to declare total war on all Russians everywhere, closing credit cards and wire transfers, phones connections, internet access to and from Russia, shutting down all Russian news and media, and weaponizing national populations to demonize, hate, and denounce Russians. According to the new ideology, Biden's New Peace Doctrine, there is only one truth to this complicated blood feud in Ukraine. We must defer to those in power, not ask questions, not think critically, and only trust, and obey for there is no other way to be happy in life but to trust and obey people in power. Without Russian or American aid, there would be no civil war in Ukraine. Without American military aid, the war would have been over in a week. Ukraine's military advances against the east have only been possible due to Western troops, whom the media still call 'advisors,' on the ground and military aid, in a nation that is important only because it borders Russia.

From the late 1990s onwards, America has been seeking to rewrite history and avoid the inevitable. America seeks global control of strategic resources to sustain its economic primacy in the world. It fears rising powers such as China and India. It is well-positioned around the world, through its network of military bases to control and direct national ruling classes and prevent competitive pressures. It effectively muzzled and disabled Japan and continues to de-industrialize Australia. America appropriates natural resources wherever they may be secured, be they in the Middle East, Russia, or South America. It is typical behavior for a nation under severe stress. Trump was a symptom of this deep malaise in America and look what happened to him.

This threat is real. America will fall. It is only a matter of time. History proves that no nation lasts forever, and there have been greater, more splendid, more incredible global superpowers in world history than America. You can see what's left of them in museums or help archaeologists dig them up in the desert sands. The American ruling class, however, wants to cheat destiny, and if they need to kill a billion people to do it, they will happily do so, provided they write the history books. Those who benefit financially from the American trade system and global architecture will simply turn a blind eye to the victims. After all, their ancestors did the same when the indigenous peoples of Canada, America, and Australia were butchered, enslaved, and persecuted.

Most people believe that America stands for freedom and democracy and that we can feel safe and secure under the protection of the United States of America, though they are hardly united. No other nation expresses so much self-loathing as America. It is as if, in some places, America is stuck in a time warp, and one expects Robert E. Lee to walk down the street. Many Americans still remember segregation, and many long for a return to those dreadful days.

While American post-war history is a slow, torturous march toward racial equality, the American state underpins prosperity at home by destroying freedom abroad. Without this vicious foreign policy, there would be no freedom in America, and the ruling class would need a different system for the accumulation of national wealth. These days, few remember Salvador Allende, the late South American leader of Chile whose democratically elected regime in 1973 was toppled by an American-designed coup to install the fascist Augusto Pinochet who ushered in a reign of terror. America also supported the dictator Chiang Kai-shek, who ruled Taiwan with an iron fist, murdering thousands. Washington was instrumental in the toppling of the democratically elected pro-Russian government in Ukraine in 2014. The eastern, pro-Russian provinces have refused to accept that coup and this laid the basis for this current conflict.

If America and Russia did not interfere in Ukraine, there would be no war. There are American bases, NATO bases, and Western troops on the ground in Ukraine, and the most biased media since the days of the Indian Mutiny. All of this makes a mockery of the fiction presented by political leaders about this war being about *'defending territorial sovereignty and integrity.'* Most nations do not possess territorial integrity or sovereignty in the current international order, as they are part of one sphere of influence or another. It is to be expected and has been normal practice for centuries. Ukraine is careful not to boast about its democracy since it doesn't exist anymore, but the West is not so nuanced, regularly justifying its war against Russia as a war between *'autocracy'* and *'democracy.'* This is strange because America supports both Egypt and Saudi Arabia as key allies. Both are autocratic regimes and will never embrace democracy. Both nations are critical to the strategic interests of American foreign policy. For some strange reason, the global western media ignores these inconsistencies, and politicians give beautiful speeches about their desire to promote democracy and freedom in Ukraine.

Democracy in our world is not about freedom, but about an alliance with America. It is code for *'we stand with America,'* or *'we are with America.'* A global economic order precludes the possibility of true territorial independence and sovereignty. Many genuine democratic nations in the world have the presence of the American military, which suggests that none of them are truly free, or sovereignly independent. Some nations have negligible forces stationed there, while others are puppet regimes which are regimes that are effectively run from Washington.

The classic puppet regime is Australia, which since the mid-1970s has never deviated from complete obedience to American foreign policy. This started with the late Harold Holt who said, *'All the Way with the LBJ,'* in 1966, but history has shown it was *'All the way with the USA.'* Except for a brief period under the nationalist Gough Whitlam in the 1970s, Australia has rarely dared to question or oppose any American policy in the region. It was Holt who approved the infamous American spy base at Pine Gap in 1966. Since then, Australia without criticism accepts whatever military base America seeks to impose on the land down under.

Australia is virtually an American protectorate, not that you would notice from the chattering classes. If you despair over the American Culture war, spare a thought for the paucity of Australian political culture. It is myopic, provincial, and drowning in pseudo-intellectualism, on a platter of overdone white supremacy. Australia copies American leadership on virtually every major foreign policy issue and then claims that it came up with the idea, which has been quite amusing over the decades. Under the previous regime of Scott Morrison, the plans were laid for the stationing of nuclear weapons in the nation's north, and American nuclear submarines along the east coast. All the while, the tiny, white-dominated political leadership boasts of Australia's *'robust and strong democracy and freedom.'*

Australia has never won a war without foreign aid and will never win a war without foreign aid and has sacrificed its independence and territorial sovereignty for generations first to England, then America, out of morbid fear that *'evil foreigners'* will come and steal the land they stole from the indigenous people in the nineteenth century. The early settlers and British troops engaged in a century-long war of genocide and conflict to brutally destroy the indigenous population and then seek their complete eradication culturally and spiritually. The Christian Church, namely the Church of England not only stood by but aided and abetted the slaughter and the misery. Unlike in America, where treaties were made and broken, there were no reservations in Australia to send the original inhabitants, only chains to wrap around their necks, hunting parties where the landed gentry went out to *'shoot blacks'* and then go to church, and generations of aboriginal women who were raped and abused. This is the nation that fears invasion. This is Australia, the land of the free down under. Australia fears that God will take retribution for what their ancestors did and which they so convincingly seek to deny ever happened.

Was it a war or genocide? If a war, then why not record the events at the War Memorial in Canberra? If that is accepted, then Australia needs to be prosecuted for war crimes since as British subjects the aboriginal people were victims of genocide during a time of war. If it was not war, then it was genocide and again it means Australia is guilty of violating territorial independence and sovereignty, the very thing it claims today to believe in. What a muddle for white supremacy down under. Surely this would be sufficient motivation to build bridges, promote peace, seek restitution, and move forward, but it is Australia, and that is hoping for a miracle.

In Australia, there was a brief glimmer of hope in the 1980s and 1990s with talk of *'Asian engagement'* and *'multiculturalism.'* The idea of many peoples living under the same law with equality, safety, and peace, was not original – it came from America - but for the old regime, the white supremacists who run Australia, it was a bold experiment. Australia is a *'wait your turn'* society based on the principle of generational racism. Only now are the children of migrants who came in the 1950s and 1960s allowed to climb up the ranks to positions of power. The rest must *'wait their turn,'* in this so-called deeply egalitarian society. The short-lived multicultural experiment was mild compared to the revolutionary efforts of African Americans to secure equality under the law, but it was a vision in the context of an America more confident in global leadership than it is today. Today, America is a full-fledged imperial state, a war economy, and its political culture is tearing itself apart due to self-loathing. Its ruling class is sadly inward-looking, and paranoid, living in a fascist paradise, run by the twin standards of mediocrity, and senility.

Will America be able to calm the fears of Australia or the world? Will America save Australia? Will America be able to secure freedom for the nations? No, no, and no. Nations do not bring freedom, they bring opportunity, but freedom comes from God. Australia was betrayed by Britain in World War Two and it is quite likely America will do the same in the future, seeking to secure its strategic interests. All of America's allies and friends are *'friends for a season,'* friends of mutual strategic interest, but there is nothing eternal or permanent about any of it. This is international relations, and it only goes as far as it can and that is not very far at all. In terms of an antidote for fear, the alliance with America is simply a distraction, not a cure.

It is not America's fault. They have a role to play in history's great drama and to a large extent, it is a received script. But only a fool would place their trust in political power. This, to many, sounds like a foolish thing to say, as so many crave power, and political power, especially in the church. Those who wield true power would say that it is fleeting and does not live up to its reputation. Those who have no faith in God are free to do as they like, they can march off to war and get blown to pieces for the ruling class. They can worship the state in Covid Hysteria as millions have done, happily injecting themselves with the latest booster while living with the constant threat of Covid.

There will always be a war somewhere and always be a form of Hysteria and propaganda. Democracies cannot exist without propaganda, or they will end up like a dictatorship, requiring political violence. Fascists in America decry the January 6 goon show and coup-lite but the *'light on a hill,'* is more like a wooden house deep in a swamp, the foundations are rotting. America seems to be sadly, on this path toward political oblivion, political chaos, and some form of civil war. After all, they have had two and the last one achieved very little. Just ask the ghost of Rutherford Hayes, a mediocre man who undid the greatness of Abe Lincoln. Few remember Hayes but he set America back generations and helped to give birth to Jim Crow and segregation.

It is perhaps because of Christianity that America speaks a lot about freedom, though, for many, it was always elusive, and worth fighting for. America captured the word freedom and in more recent years, has made it synonymous with democracy, which in turn, as I have said, is code for a nation run by America. But democracy and freedom are not the same, they never have been. Freedom is ancient. Freedom is like a sea of flowers that spreads across the world and America has picked up one flower in the sea and claimed patent rights over all of them. America has no right to do so, nor does any nation. American freedom is sterile not because it is American but because it is based on what humans promise each other, and for that reason alone, it is not true freedom. It is a lie. Freedom comes from God and God alone.

Political power has always been a problem for Christians, especially those who have given up on Christ. The Christian Fascist is the person who seeks to mix faith and flag in some way, using political power to build a kingdom on earth in the name of God. It is in name only, of course, they have no intention of following Christ, or listening to God. The Christian Fascist knows the power that comes with politics and for them, it is not about the grace and mercy of God found in the Lord Jesus Christ, a personal faith, a transforming faith by the Holy Spirit, but it is a nation that exercises power like all humans do, with fear and punishment.

What is the antidote to fear?

The Christian Fascist places their faith, not in God but in institutions, rules, and political power. They replace one fear with another. Who decides citizenship in this kind of nation? A religious court? A spiritual tribunal? I believe that there is an antidote to fear, and it seems to me when we are seeking freedom from fear that the only place we can go, is God. He is the only one who can overcome fear. It is a simple thing to say, and it is a simple thing to believe. We live in a world where we are told to fear one thing and then another, and then another. The goal of this insanity is to trust the government without questioning them in any way. This is a parody of faith and yes, it is demonic. Many churches are now evangelists for the government and use the pulpit to push sectarian agendas. In many ways, they always were. From Congress to the pulpit or from the courts to the church, it is simply pushing human power from one arena to the next. Political power is human power, and it has its limits.

The antidote to fear is speaking to God. That is the starting point. The church is not the place to go. He is not there waiting for you. It is his world and God's presence is everywhere. Speaking to God can be part of our daily life. Prayer need not be something special we wait to do each week, but a daily reality in our life, as common as breathing. Without breath, we cannot live and without speaking to God we cannot survive.

True Christianity only begins with genuine prayer and the reading of the scripture. Any idiot can go to church and many do. It is easy to be a Christian at church, the bar is so low, that even the Devil could turn up and be made a churchwarden. It is only when faith becomes personal that it becomes real. This is not what the church teaches of course. The church has become a drug for Christians. Dare I quote Marx and say that church has become the opium of Christians to the extent that the church has become one's default faith? Most Christians I have met over the years cannot survive without their local church which means they have no faith, or they have such little faith that it is impossible to tell the difference. The action of the faith occurs outside the church building. That is where life is and faith in action. It is not at church.

You know church people, they look the same and they smell the same, and it is not a good look, and we all know that Church smell. It is the odor of false piety, the aroma of self-righteousness. They believe that simply turning up on Sunday is all that is needed to follow God. They believe that going through the rituals will bring extra blessings in heaven. But the person of faith is the one who brings God into all their life.

While the antidote to fear is prayer, it comes with a cost. It is not pretty. It is real. Prayer only becomes real when we are praising God, not simply asking him for something. This is what he says:

'Rejoice in the Lord always. I will say it again: Rejoice! Let your gentleness be evident to all. The Lord is near. Do not be anxious about anything, but in every situation, by prayer and petition, with thanksgiving, present your requests to God. And the peace of God, which transcends all understanding, will guard your hearts and your minds in Christ Jesus' (Philippians 4: 4-7).

It is easy to say that we should pray. Indeed, it is more difficult to pray. It is even more difficult to pray rejoicing, especially in difficult times. But it is in those times that faith becomes real and not just something we claim to believe in. It becomes something that burns into our hearts through the trials of life. We do not rejoice, as Paul says, in our misery. For example, we do not say *'thank God I am suffering, thank God I am in misery or sadness,'* only a fool would say these things and Paul is no fool. But what he is saying is that we are to rejoice in the Lord. We are to rejoice in the Lord Jesus Christ.

The test of our faith during times of fear, pain, and trial is not to blindly face the misery stoically but to do so rejoicing in the Lord Jesus Christ. Christ reminds us of what has happened, the big picture if you will, of our life, the big picture of our salvation, our hope for the future, and our assurances of eternal life. But it is not simply the big picture, it is the big picture framing the details of our lives so that this rejoicing in Christ is what we carry in our daily life, in our daily walk.

We rejoice in the Lord because he is worth rejoicing over for what he has done is a matter for rejoicing. Sadly, many who claim to follow Jesus never talk about him, and they never talk about faith because they don't have any. They spend most of their time in sectarian warfare or engaged in the Culture War. Paul urges us to be gentle. This is in close association with rejoicing and prayer and so it must be deliberate. Paul was not a theologian but a brilliant thinker who did not say things by accident. Gentleness. This is one of the fruits of the Spirit. But why link rejoicing and prayer with gentleness? Joyous people are gentle people and gentle people are people of prayer. I think it is that simple.

It does not mean effeminate or weak, nor does it mean having weak handshakes or soft voices. Anyone can have the spirit of gentleness. What is interesting is that Paul tells us that our gentleness is to be known to all people. That is, our spirit of gentleness is to be public, not to be private or secret, but public. I have met few men or women of a gentle spirit in public life so we can easily exclude them as being those who follow Christ. It also includes most church leaders. Most are not gentle, they are factious, divisive, hateful, and bitter. These days the church is involved in bitter factional disputes or arguing with governments over their need for more money and political power.

The West's Paedophile God

Tell me how many children came to faith in Christ in the New Testament? Very few. The Western Church is obsessed with children. It is a sickness. It is an illness. In 2,000 years of Christianity, genuine faith is made later in life, or it matures later in life, and while many come to faith when they are kids, most give up because their faith was never genuine. Christian Fascists point to the prison warden in Acts. Yes, his whole household came to faith, including grandpa and grandma and the household slaves. Christian Fascists point to Timothy. Pastor Tim was a man, not a child.

The national churches treated baptism as a form of citizenship. For many nations, this was synonymous with being a member of a church. Most kids who are baptized want nothing to do with Jesus Christ later in life. The modern Christian education program has been a failure and has produced millions of Christian Fascists, who in turn, want to force people to believe in their version of God. We see this in the desire to send children to religious schools to receive the Christian values their parents fail to give at home. Many Christians believe that the only ones who will accept the faith are children, and so they have kids programs and Sunday Schools and Youth Groups, but God is not a paedophile and he does not single out children, no that is the church. God seeks people of all ages, and nowhere in the Bible does he prefer children. The pivot towards education for the church was one of the worst decisions the West has made in centuries. They did it for money of course – many of the religious schools are profitable, unlike churches themselves, but religious schools are the training grounds for fascists. I am not talking about the ancient elite religious schools that have been around for centuries. Everyone knows they are *'Christian'* in name only, but I am talking about the modern belief in the mass education of children with *'Christian values,'* whatever they are. Many of these schools are not unlike the Taliban camps that we hear so much about and condemn. Christian Fascists are opposed to the gospel of Jesus Christ, which is about a new heart, not new behavior. God does not convert through education or government declaration.

You will look in vain to find gentleness in Christian Fascism be it the inculcated nonsense of school values or the ritualized nonsense of church religion. True gentleness is a work of God's Holy Spirit in the heart of a person, the only true change available to all of us. Let us ask God for more gentleness in our world, step out in faith and be gentle, one day at a time, whilst following Jesus.

The children, well, they are in God's hands, let the little children come unto me says Christ, and do not hinder them for such are those in the kingdom of God (Matthew 19: 14). Jesus did not say, keep the gay kids away please, the kingdom of God is only for straight boys and girls. No, that would be the church. This gentleness of spirit in the life of a Christian is important. Children were attracted to Jesus. He did not scare them. Children trusted him. Only the diehard fanatics, religious lunatics, Christian Fascists, (and sadly) many vulnerable people and liars trust the church now.

It is sad, it is an indictment, it is a tragedy that the Christian Church has become an institution known for child abuse. Instead of turning away from this terrible evil, the Churches have fought it every step of the way. Now they pretend as if it never happened and have turned their attention to children again, this time under the guise of protecting them from gender fluidity. They want to stop gay kids and transgender kids and all kinds of kids really from identifying with one or more genders. Listen, it is the same church and the same people and the same brutality, ready for the next generation. Don't you think the church has done enough damage to children or do you want another generation of lawsuits? Leave the children alone for the sake of the kids and the gospel and for the sake of the name of God which they have dragged through the mud for so long.

So, we are to rejoice and be gentle and we are to bring our prayers and petitions to God. Importantly, Paul tells us that we are not to be anxious, we are not to be anxious about anything at all. It is easy to say, but not easy to do. Anxiety follows many of us like our shadows. How can we leave anxiety behind? I believe it is a discipline, it is a practice to be learned, and it is not automatic. For some of us, it will be a struggle, but God is with us, even in our anxiety, and our pain, in some ways, he is even more present in those times. We are to present our requests and prayers to God, to make them known to him. We need to verbalize them and tell them to God.

Paul ends with a promise that will come to all who pray: *'and the peace of God which passes all understanding, will guard your heart and mind in Christ Jesus.'* This makes sense because we are praying through Jesus to the Father, and we are in Him. This peace of God is from God and of God and it is so wonderful that it is beyond the mind and beyond all understanding. What is the antidote to fear? It is praying, while rejoicing in the Lord, with a gentle spirit evident to all. This is how fear is defeated in the life of a Christian in a world that hates those who follow Jesus.

How does God understand fear?

Most people fear something. Many things are quite legitimate. Parents fear for their children especially when they are young. Children often lack street sense, or common sense, skills that one can learn over time. We also seem to have an intuitive sense of fear, or awareness of our surroundings. We avoid danger or dangerous situations and so we should. It is quite natural. We fear authority and representatives of authority, such as the police or the tax office. A nation needs rules, and they are there for the purpose of order and organization. Many children fear their parents or accept their authority over them. Many parents have different ways to raise their children, and most kids have a healthy respect for their parents, or at least aspire to.

How does God understand fear? The way God understands fear is like the way our dictionaries understand fear. In other words, there is no special difference between the way we understand the anatomy of fear and the way the Bible understands it and presents it. The Bible has three ways of understanding fear which in Greek is *'Phobos,'* which is where we get our word phobia. In my Greek Lexicon of the New Testament, the New Testament first speaks of the state of being frightened, afraid, and apprehensive. In this, is included the ideas of terror and intimidation. Second, fear of someone or something. Third, having deep respect and reverence for someone.

The same Greek word is used for all three categories. There are many examples in the New Testament where all three ways of the word phobia are used. Sometimes the translators adapt to the context to provide deeper clarity in the text, sometimes they don't and sometimes their decisions make little sense in the context, though they probably have their reasons.

It is the same in English, but we tend to associate fear with a negative persona. Our language has changed dramatically in the last century and fear is one of them. In Greek, the usage of the word is usually found in the context. We would normally say to our children or to children, *'you need to have proper respect for authority,'* rather than *'you need to be afraid of the police.'*

Likewise, we would use the word *'afraid'* to offer comfort to people in need or anxiety. For example, we would say *'there is no need to be afraid of the dark,'* or whatever it happens to be. Again, to use the children's example, we would caution children to be careful in the yard, and look out for spiders or snakes or whatever, we would not tell them to fear spiders or snakes, though we might tell them to have proper respect for them and be aware of their existence and behavior. We tend not to try and instill fear in people.

We probably would not use the word *'fear.'* Fear these days is an old-fashioned word, like naughty, which once meant evil and now it means mischievous. Even our word *'evil'* seems too soft for some of the crimes today. Language is always changing. We might call someone *'fearless,'* meaning brave or courageous, often used for a soldier or even a sporting hero on the field. We also use the word phobia more often even though this now points to a habit or a psychological condition, such as Islamophobia, common in America during the War on Terror, or Homophobia, or Xenophobia.

Unfortunately, many people, including many Christians, tend to be unaware of the three types of using fear in the New Testament. Christians often like the word *'fear'* and it often fits with the way we want to see God or rather, the way, we want others to see God. How does God understand fear? I often hear Christians say that we have lost a sense of the fear of God or that we need to renew our fear of God, and they insist on the use of the word fear, which itself poses a problem not only for interpretation but also for implication. It certainly doesn't mean that we should not fear anything and be fearless in all things. *Freedom Matters Today* investigates and researches important contemporary topics from a Christian perspective. We try to point people back to the Bible, and a personal rather than institutional relationship with God.

But it is also important to think clearly about things and fear is one of those things that we need to think clearly about. We seek to see more clearly how fear relates to the Christian life, focusing attention on a Biblical understanding of fear and the dismantling of fake fear or constructed manufactured fears and anxieties. Many new fears have emerged in our society due to the rise of this new form of politics, such as Covid Hysteria, and WW3. These are manufactured fear, cultivated fears, and fears created by the ruling class for the purposes of social control.

At stake, it seems to be a question of political authority, and as America falls slowly into history, the ruling class is desperate and through the exploitation of fear seeks to garner our absolute obedience. We in the West worship the nation, which is a tragedy, and it is also a sin. It is idolatry. Nation worship is common among Western Christians for some reason. I can only assume it is because of Christian Fascism, the hankering after the reimagined and fictitious Christian past. We ought not to fear the nation, our nation, or any nation. They are simply a pool from which God draws his people to faith in Christ. Beyond that, the nations, are free. Thank God. Therefore, to properly address the anatomy of fear in the life of a person, we need to understand the Bible's perspective on politics to overthrow manufactured fear and anxiety. We have already looked at two. The first is national destiny and the second is free speech. The third is citizenship. In examining national destiny, speech, and citizenship, we can understand a Christian's identity in the world and through this, rejoice in the freedom God gives us.

Many believe that America is a Christian nation and that it has a destiny or a role to play in God's great salvation. I pointed out that there is no evidence in the Bible that God favors one of the nations, outside of Israel. We in the nations, the so-called Gentile nations, bring nothing to God. The problem is fascism and Christians who long for the old days when the church held the sword. The mixing of faith and flag is not new, nor is it confined to America. Are there special nations? No. Is America exceptional? No. Do nations have a destiny? No.

How does God understand fear? He does not need America. Many Christians would be deeply offended by these assertions, and this is a problem. They suffer from a form of idol worship and America has replaced God in their actual belief. It is the flowering of the sin of Christian Fascism. It happens everywhere. Many nations have invented Christian traditions where the future of their nation and Christianity are intertwined. These are based on a false misreading of the Hebrew Bible and the transplanting of the privileges of Israel to whichever nation they come from.

If God does not bless America, I believe this presents a wonderful opportunity for America to pursue its own destiny, rather than be confined by the fanatical ramblings of Christian Fascists and their ilk. This would be true freedom. God does not control nations like a puppet master with strings. The nations are the source of those who come to faith in the Savior Jesus Christ. How does God understand fear? He doesn't need nations to fit in with his program or use their fear machines to do his work.

We are only truly free when we speak to God. I pointed out that there is no such thing as free speech, and that Christians are to be people who guard their tongues rather than engage in damaging slander and gossip. I don't expect to make much difference here since gossip is the reason many go to church on Sundays. More importantly, it is because of the work of Jesus on the cross, dying in our place, for our sins, that he opened the possibility for us to enter the presence of God and speak openly and clearly to God about our feelings, desires, and needs. True free speech is only before God.

Our citizenship is in heaven, it is not on earth, and we are to seek the kingdom of God, not an earthly kingdom. *'My kingdom is not of this world,'* says Jesus. Christian Fascists close their Bible and invent their own sick, and twisted views of God. Paul says in Philippians 3: 20: *'But our citizenship is in heaven. And we eagerly await a Savior from there, the Lord Jesus Christ.'* This will conclude our discussion on Christian politics and how to understand the relationship between faith and flag.

What is your equilibrium?

What is our default position, our starting point? I mean by this, when we are settled as people, how are we? What is our baseline? What is your equilibrium? In life, some people are content, some people are discontent, and some people are angry. Some people never get angry. Nothing seems to unsettle them.

I don't know about you, but lots of Christians I meet are angry people. I have been to dozens of churches over the years all over the world, and the more you see, the less you see, the more people you meet the fewer types of people you meet. You see it in their stares, you see it in the way they look at other people, you see it in the way they talk to their friends and avoid their enemies. Many church people might be polite, and to some degree friendly, but underneath there is a seething fury, a deep resentment, anxiety, and rage. They rage at the world, they rage at each other, and they rage at all the people they hold responsible for the evils in their generation. Underneath it all, they rage against God.

I am not talking about anger derived from the current political, economic, or social chaos. After ruining the economy through disastrous lockdowns and idiotic public health policies that hardly deserve the name, the ruling class refuses to talk about Covid, even though more people in Australia die each day at the end of 2022 from the disease than at the height of the martial law lockdowns. This was a disgraceful time when churches implemented vaccine passports, police arrested and beat people not wearing masks, and sent armed anti-terrorist troops to break up peaceful protests of ordinary people who were suffering. Now, Covid waves continue to crash through the Australian community and the corrupt ruling class lets it run rampant, deceitfully saying *'it's back to business as usual,'* and nonchalantly insisting on the next booster shot of a 'vaccine' that cannot stop the spread, cannot prevent transmission, cannot prevent serious illness, and cannot prevent death. If after all the death, all the political lies, all the deceit, all the corruption, you still believe the government never lied to you, and that the politicians and the health bureaucrats always have your best interests at heart, then I am sorry, then is not much hope for you because you will believe anything now. You probably think that *'Stand with Ukraine'* is about right and wrong, about good versus evil. If you think that Australian foreign policy is righteous, investigate their policies on East Timor. If you think America is righteous, investigate the history of Agent Orange.

War is about money, not morality, it is about business, not bodies, it is about accounts, not accountability. The war in Ukraine is a business war, and a testing ground for new technology with the people of Ukraine – mainly the poor who could not fly out to the West – as target practice. It echoes Italy's invasion of Ethiopia (1935-7) and is almost a complete re-run of the Korean War. The war is basically about fulfilling contractual obligations to weapons manufacturers in America and Europe following the end of the 20-year wars in the Middle East. America's departure from Kabul was like Saigon, a complete mess. Millions of Americans depend on these contracts. Expectations have been raised for 20 years due to America's love of war and this expectation-driven business cycle compels the state to find wars and at least pretend it is all for a good cause rather than a vicious cycle of unproductive investment on a massive scale.

Both Covid and WW3 as major crises drive much of the contrived political fears of the day. It is not about democracy or freedom, but money and power. We can always get angry about this or about Covid Hysteria and WW3, but you should not be surprised when people in power get going. They always do the same thing – just read a bit of history – there is always some group to benefit financially from war, and they are usually the ones who start it, and run it. When Jesus was asked about the end times he says, *'well, there will be wars,'* and he is right, there always are, and always will be.

The Cultural Wars are also in full swing now in America and her satellites such as Australia and Canada and these drive anger. It is the season, not to be jolly, but to be angry. Christian Fascists and their friends are driven by anger and will tear society apart. In America, this insanity is at full throttle. The topics that we have been told to fill our minds over include gun control, abortion, same-sex marriage, gender fluidity, Donald Trump, transgenderism, and elections. This culture of fear and anxiety is counterproductive.

I am not talking here about political anger, but personal anger, frustration, and anxiety. A lot of Christians are simply, very angry people. I don't know why really. I suppose it is the fruit of a lifetime of poor teaching or leadership. God does not promise what he does not promise. If we rest on his promises we have comfort, security, and hope, but if not, then we walk alone, quite alone. Most Christians spend their lives fretting over things God never promised them and then they live with deep resentment. It is not surprising. We get downright disturbed if we go to church and see someone happy. We think *'what is wrong with this guy?'* We become suspicious. What most people are thinking is *'I hope he doesn't try and sit in my seat'*, or *'I hope he doesn't come and talk to me.'*

I read about a book promoting Christian heritage in Australia. What heritage? The book is a work of fiction, a fantasy, speaking about how Christianity shaped modern Australia. Which Christianity was this? Up until the present era, most churches hated each other. They loathed each other, especially Protestants and Catholics. If you talk to the seriously devoted fascists in the Church of Rome, the hatred is still there, and it is still there in all the major Protestant denominations in Australia. All churches are full of divisions and enmities. Even today, this enmity is deep, even within denominations or church societies.

There is the story of a man who is found alone on a deserted island in the ocean and on the island, there are three buildings. He is asked by the captain of the boat what they were, and he first points out his home and then the church he attends. The captain asks about the final building and the man reluctantly tells him that this was the church he used to go to.

Our default position as Christians is not anger, but it is to rejoice in the Lord. What is our starting point as Christians? Well, Paul tells us simply that we are to rejoice in the Lord (Philippians 3:1). Rejoice in the Lord? Wow. What a recommendation! What is he saying here exactly? It is very interesting to unpack what he is saying in the verse. It is very surprising. Paul is not saying to be happy for the sake of being happy. He is not saying to put on a face and hope for the best or put on a fake smile.

The word rejoice in Greek is not optional, it is not a suggestion, it is an imperative. This is something we must do. It is in the present imperative active – we must do this now, not tomorrow, but now. It means to rejoice as we understand it, to be glad. The word is also closely associated with the Greek word for grace as well as joy, which is undeserved favor, so it is perhaps why Paul uses this word rejoice as it suggests graciousness, a joyful spirit, all connected with the person and work of the Holy Spirit.

Paul was in prison when he wrote Philippians so it makes sense that the only way he could rejoice was because God was already in his heart – the fruit of the Spirit – so this is not wishful thinking or optimism in the face of danger, bravado, but a settled sense of joy, continual joy. But furthermore, it is not simply having a sense of joy or gladness or a spirit of rejoicing. Most Christians would leave it there and say that Christians are happy people, or they have that inner peace, whatever that means. No, we are to rejoice in the Lord. Who is the Lord? Jesus. Lord means Master, king. Our equilibrium position is to rejoice in the Master Jesus. This is our starting point. As king, he is our Lord, and he has our back, he fights for us and he fought for us, and we do not fear.

What is the Christian's greatest danger?

What is the Christian's greatest danger? It seems to me that the greatest danger to the Christian is not extremes, but the ordinary. Since Christian Fascists run the churches in the West, they are always out to get someone. It is typical church behavior. It is why these hypocrites are so popular. When you are being persecuted simply for believing in the name of the Lord Jesus Christ, extremes soon disappear. We struggle with the everyday.

Once I traveled around Japan with a full set of luggage. These bags were heavy. So, each day, I lightened my load shirt by shirt, thing by thing, until after a week, I had very little left, only what I needed. My journey thereafter was sweet and eventful, and I did not remember what I had left behind in the past.

Jesus was tempted by the Devil not during his confrontations with the Pharisees, nor even at Gethsemane, but when he was hungry. This ordinary moment in his life was the time when Satan sought to bring him down. Matthew 4:1-4 records that:

'Then Jesus was led by the Spirit into the wilderness to be tempted by the devil. After fasting for forty days and forty nights, he was hungry. The tempter came to him and said, "If you are the Son of God, tell these stones to become bread. Jesus answered, "It is written: 'Man shall not live on bread alone, but on every word that comes from the mouth of God."'

It was at his moment of human weakness, that he was tempted. Jesus makes a similar point in one of his sermons when he talks about money. Money is a thing, and we need it to live because it is the currency for the buying and selling of commodities. But it can become a burden to us. Jesus said in Matthew 6: 19-21:

'Do not store up for yourselves treasures on earth, where moths and vermin destroy, and where thieves break in and steal. But store up for yourselves treasures in heaven, where moths and vermin do not destroy, and where thieves do not break in and steal. For where your treasure is, there your heart will be also.

Paul says much the same thing in Philippians. It is the desire to wrap your spirituality in some package for all to see which at his heart is the danger for anyone who seeks to follow Jesus. Something external, something mundane becomes central and the way to distinguish life from death.

In the first century, many rituals signified a kind of lifestyle and value system of faith. One of them for men was circumcision, which was the cutting of the foreskin of the penis. This was not exceptional – everyone had it done. It was to identify with the nation of Israel, it was a nod to the traditions, the customs all Jews observed. Every male Jew was circumcised. It was religious, it was national, it was custom. It was everyday and mundane.

Paul opposed it, even though he was circumcised himself, he saw no reason why anyone believing in Christ needed to be. It didn't matter how common it was, how ordinary it was, Paul saw in the attitude of those insisting upon it a kind of thinking about themselves and God that was repulsive. It was the work of man not the work of God, it was the insistence that something man did made a person right with God, it was the idea that all that mattered was someone ordinary that everyone had which meant no one needed to grow in relation to God. Paul writes in Philippians 3: 1-6:

'It is no trouble for me to write the same things to you again, and it is a safeguard for you. Watch out for those dogs, those evildoers, those mutilators of the flesh. For it is we who are the circumcision, we who serve God by his Spirit, who boast in Christ Jesus, and who put no confidence in the flesh. Though I have reasons for such confidence. If someone else thinks they have reasons to put confidence in the flesh, I have more: circumcised on the eighth day of the people of Israel, of the tribe of Benjamin, a Hebrew of Hebrews; regarding the law, a Pharisee; as for zeal, persecuting the church; as for righteousness based on the law, faultless.'

What these men in the circumcision group were saying was that *'yes you can believe in Jesus, but you must also get your foreskin cut.'* If you did that, you were right with God, you were now a citizen of God's kingdom, you were right with God, and all was right with you. It was easily done, and with one flick of the knife, you could enjoy all the privileges of being a member of the nation of Israel. All you needed to do was simply join the club, sit back, and enjoy your new relationship with God because you have changed your citizenship from a foreigner to a man that God accepted.

The Christian Fascists who turned Christianity into the church did the same with infant baptism. For centuries, Christian Fascists taught that baptism ushered you into the kingdom of God, the sprinkling of water regenerated your soul, and the blessing of the priest made you right with God even if you had no faith whatsoever. Yes, one day you needed to believe, but proof of your faith was baptism. It was essential.

This is the same with the gay and transgender debates in the church. The fascists say *'yes, believe in Jesus but you must also agree that the only marriage God allows is between a man and a woman.'* Some even say that *'yes, believe in Jesus but you must be heterosexual because God only loves heterosexual people.'* This is not the gospel. This is a false gospel. Paul is condemning this attitude because it is the celebration of what we do rather than what God has done. Paul is severe in his criticism – he calls these people *'dogs'* a harsh criticism even in our day – to emphasize that they are separate from the life of God. They celebrate what he calls the flesh, the religious cravings of people, the desire to make us right with God, the efforts to lift ourselves to heaven by doing something ordinary and mundane – a flick of the knife, or in baptism, a sprinkle of the water, or a statement about marriage.

Confidence in these rituals deadens faith and deadens a life with God. Nothing that we can do in our lives can change our relationship with God. These rituals mean nothing as far as God is concerned. Even in circumcision, it was a ritual to confirm pre-existing membership to the nation of Israel, as one was, and still is born a Jew, into the Jewish nation. Paul was adamant that even though he was a Jew of Jews, he refused to place any confidence in the flesh, in his human efforts to make himself right with God. Instead, he boldly claims for both Jews and non-Jews, *'For it is we who are the circumcision, we who serve God by his Spirit, who boast in Christ Jesus, and who put no confidence in the flesh.'*

In other words, those who are set apart are not set apart by the works of a man, with a flick of a knife, but by the work of God, his Spirit, in our hearts. The real work is done by God, not us. The reason for our confidence is not ourselves but the work of another, the Lord Jesus Christ, in whom we are to rejoice. We all serve God by his Spirit, no matter our earthly nation or ethnicity for our boast is in God.

What is the heart of faith?

A man or woman of faith has faith in Christ, not in themselves. That is the heart of the Christian Gospel, the good news. We have faith in another person. Faith is not saying that we are useless or incapable, but it is saying that in terms of knowing God and being known by God, we need to go beyond ourselves. Faith has to do with another person rather than us. Faith is about trust, it is about acceptance, it is about a new beginning. If we know Jesus, or if we decide to follow Jesus, the heart of faith is a recognition that we are in a relationship with God by virtue of another, not ourselves, and that one is the Lord Jesus Christ. It is because of the identity and actions of Jesus in living a life of morality that we could not, and by dying for our sin, on our behalf, that we can be confident of the one in whom we place our trust.

This attitude may not be immediately apparent for a Christian since there are so many voices competing for their attention. A Christian we are told is someone who goes to a church building on Sunday, joins a club of Christians, called a denomination, and sets aside time and money to cultivate that investment. It involves loyalty to that group, baptism, and the right language. Over time, family affiliation is involved and often national loyalties so eventually one is convinced that being a Christian is defined by ritualistic participation in a weekly church service, or that it is something we actively do, and without these actions, then we are not Christians.

Most Christians think like this in the West. The old word for this was *'earthly-minded.'* It has its focus downwards, towards the earth, towards human traditions, man-made conventions and expectations, and what people expect and demand. Even today, many have religious convictions because of another, be it spouse or parents, friends, or community expectations. A cursory reading of the New Testament reveals that early Christians or followers of Jesus struggled with the very things we believe today are the reasons behind the fall of Christian witness, the rise of the so-called *'post-Christian'* society.

Society was never, nor is it, nor will it be Christian. Peter would not tell his readers to avoid malice, deceit, envy, slander, or hypocrisy if they did not themselves struggle as all do with these things (1 Peter 2: 1). The obsession with the earth, reputation, what others think and value, what we call 'consumer culture,' had its equivalents in the ancient world, they were not very different from us at all. It was in the days of Paul and the apostles, even in the beginning of the Christian faith. Even the best fruit are vulnerable to pests. Fruit trees grown a thousand years ago in Palestine are no different from fruit trees grown in California, the struggles are the same, the problems are the same, and the fruit, by and large, is the same. It is the same with people.

The way of the Christian is the opposite. If you are following the expectations of the church, the denomination, the traditions, the rituals, the heritage, then you are on the wrong path, for you are not following the Spirit, you are not opening your eyes to brothers and sisters in Christ across the aisle in the other churches or other denominations, who have an equal share in your faith, and with whom you will share eternity. It is not you or your traditions that bind people together, it is God who binds people together by his Spirit. The source of our boasting or the basis for our confidence is not ourselves but it is the person of Jesus Christ. Paul writes in Philippians 3: 7-11:

'But whatever were gains to me I now consider loss for the sake of Christ. What is more, I consider everything a loss because of the surpassing worth of knowing Christ Jesus my Lord, for whose sake I have lost all things. I consider them garbage, that I may gain Christ and be found in him, not having a righteousness of my own that comes from the law, but that which is through faith in Christ—the righteousness that comes from God based on faith. I want to know Christ—yes, to know the power of his resurrection and participation in his sufferings, becoming like him in his death, and so, somehow, attaining to the resurrection from the dead.'

I do not believe that Paul discovered all this immediately. His was a spiritual journey and so is ours. We do not suddenly happen upon Christ in faith, and all is revealed. We grow in our understanding, not of the traditions, or the rules, or canon law, or denominational loyalty, but in our understanding of Jesus Christ. Paul says: *'I want to know Christ,'* and further, he wants to *'know the power of his resurrection.'* He wants to grow in his understanding of God and deepen his relationship with Christ every day. Paul is not always looking back and saying: *'thank God I was circumcised on the eighth day or thank God I was baptized, and I can sit here and think nothing and sit in church and say nothing and listen to the sermon and do nothing.'* Paul's faith is living, it is expressed through a genuine desire to grow, to learn, to ponder, and to experience the fullness of this wonder that is Christ.

You cannot compare Christ with anything or anyone. There was a time when all his earthly credentials meant everything to him. Paul was an intelligent man, a learned man, a wise man, that much is clear from the New Testament. Yet he could say:

'...whatever were gains to me I now consider loss for the sake of Christ. What is more, I consider everything a loss because of the surpassing worth of knowing Christ Jesus my Lord, for whose sake I have lost all things. I consider them garbage, that I may gain Christ and be found in him.'

You will not hear of a Christian Fascist say this or a Christian Nationalist. You will not hear them even mention the name of Jesus – they will talk about traditions and culture and other things but never their personal relationship with Christ – because they do not have any. Listen to the words he uses – *'loss'* – he uses it twice, and *'garbage'* contrasting the best of Paul with the simple knowledge of the Lord Jesus Christ. To know Christ says Paul, is *'surpassing worth,'* and his goal in life is that *'I may gain Christ and be found in him.'* This is faith in action.

Faith is more than simply knowing Christ – it is receiving Christ and Paul talks about this when he speaks of righteousness. This is the death blow to earthly-mindedness, the kill shot to Christian Fascism, the last nail in the coffin to self-righteousness. Receiving Christ is the heart of faith, owning faith, making it personal. This many Christians fail to ever do this, and I do not know why. They claim to believe in Jesus as their Lord and Savior and then they go through life in their own strength and in their own power. They say they receive Christ, and maybe they do – I am not going to judge them – only God knows – but what Paul says here is what every Christian must and can say: *'I may gain Christ and be found in him, not having a righteousness of my own that comes from the law, but that which is through faith in Christ—the righteousness that comes from God based on faith.'*

The righteousness of a Christian is not from within – it is not being a good person or trying to be good or holy or living a good life – but it is the righteousness of God that comes through faith in

Christ. It is through our faith in Jesus Christ, and our trust in him that we receive the righteousness of God. This does not come from the law but from God.

But Paul goes further and so must we. He is not content with simply trusting and receiving Christ. He does not want to rest on his laurels as we might say, but he wants to deepen his relationship not with the church, or with church traditions, or the church fathers, but with Christ – he wants to know Christ. *'I want to know Christ—yes, to know the power of his resurrection and participation in his sufferings, becoming like him in his death, and so, somehow, attaining to the resurrection from the dead.'* Yes, you heard correctly, he wants to know the power of the resurrection and participate in the sufferings of Christ becoming like him in his death. What does he mean by this shocking statement?

Should Christians want to suffer for Jesus?

Is persecution inevitable? Should Christians want to suffer for Jesus? This is a question that is commonly asked and poorly understood. Christian Fascists will say that if you can take over the state, then you can make sure that Christians can be protected from persecution. This temptation usually proves too much for the church and history has shown that sooner or later, they end up murdering people for not accepting their version of the institutional church.

Outside the nightmare of organized religious experience, or Christian Fascism, should Christians want to suffer for Jesus? I don't think the answer is yes in the sense that anyone woke up one day and decided to suffer for Christ out of a sense of obligation. Suffering simply happened because of their allegiance with the Lord Jesus Christ, identifying with him in his death and resurrection. There is a little bit of bravado early on before the arrival of Stephen in the Book of Acts, but once the violent persecution began led by men like Paul took form, the prophecies of Jesus about the servant not being greater than the master must have been keenly felt.

When faced with certain martyrdom in later generations under some of the Roman persecutions, no doubt a culture of martyrs developed. It became fashionable to die for the faith when faced with certain death. Most of these early stories are so overlaid with hagiography that separating fact from fiction is difficult. The creation of the martyr and hagiography was also at the heart of the religious wars between Protestants and Catholics over the last five centuries or so, especially in Europe.

Paul himself did not seek death, though he was tempted as he said once in the same letter, whether to resign himself to death or stay to encourage his disciples: *'I am torn between the two: I desire to depart and be with Christ, which is better by far'* (Philippians 1: 23). Paul was in prison for his faith in Christ.

Paul's understanding of faith was not based on himself or anything that he did, but on what Christ had done for him. As a result, he wanted to receive Christ and wanted the righteousness of God through faith. Even so, Paul wanted to go forward seeking to know Christ more. He wrote: *'I want to know Christ—yes, to know the power of his resurrection and participation in his sufferings, becoming like him in his death, and so, somehow, attaining to the resurrection from the dead.'*

This sounds a lot like Paul was looking for trouble and trying to find it. I don't think he was. Are Christians to look for persecution? No, but if they follow Christ, they will always find it. Indeed, faithfulness to the person and work of Jesus will reap persecution and it will often be from the Church.

Are Christians looking for persecution? Christians today in the West like to think they are always being persecuted and it is always unwarranted, and unfair, and that all Christians are innocent of the charges laid against them. Maybe they have their head in the sand or are just plain stupid. Anyone who has any understanding of the role of the church in the West in the last generation would be aware of the many deep failings of the Christian Church. The myth of the *'innocent church syndrome'* has only grown in the last decade. Many Christians refuse to accept any criticism of the Church and will defend the indefensible at all costs. Even after Covid Hysteria, the sin of Covid Theology, and the obscenity of the church vaccine passports, many Christians remain convinced that no charge against the church is warranted.

At seminary, I was regularly told that everyone in the world was out to get us, to persecute us, and destroy the work of the gospel. This was why we had to support any corporate venture that promoted Christian values such as religious schools. I could not understand the logic. It is a bit more complicated than that. Most of the criticisms against the church stand up to evidence, plain and simple. In addition, we need to consider the actions of political leaders who claim to act on behalf of God, especially in America. American foreign policy contributes indirectly to much of the persecution of Christian assemblies around the world, partly by the guilt of association, especially in nations that are on the receiving end of what some used to call the *'Crusader Nations.'*

The Bible anticipates suffering for Christ as normal, to be expected, and part of the Christian experience. All the New Testament writers concurred. Paul writes in Romans 5: 1-5:

'Therefore, since we have been justified through faith, we have peace with God through our Lord Jesus Christ, through whom we have gained access by faith into this grace in which we now stand. And we boast in the hope of the glory of God. Not only so, but we also glory in our sufferings, because we know that suffering produces perseverance; perseverance, character; and character, hope. And hope does not put us to shame, because God's love has been poured out into our hearts through the Holy Spirit, who has been given to us.'

Peter wrote in 1 Peter 4: 12- 16:

'Dear friends, do not be surprised at the fiery ordeal that has come on you to test you, as though something strange was happening to you. But rejoice since you participate in the sufferings of Christ, so that you may be overjoyed when his glory is revealed. If you are insulted because of the name of Christ, you are blessed, for the Spirit of glory and of God rests on you. If you suffer, it should not be as a murderer or thief or any other kind of criminal, or even as a meddler. However, if you suffer as a Christian, do not be ashamed, but praise God that you bear that name.'

James wrote in 5: 10-11:

'Brothers and sisters, as an example of patience in the face of suffering, take the prophets who spoke in the name of the Lord. As you know, we count as blessed those who have persevered. You have

heard of Job's perseverance and have seen what the Lord finally brought about. The Lord is full of compassion and mercy.'

Suffering for Christ has always been part of Christianity. Suffering for faith in Christ was commonplace in the first few centuries of Christianity. Once Christianity became a national religion, persecution tended to fade away but there were some counter-movements to return to the past paganism from time to time. Google it. It was a bit of a rollercoaster ride for Western Christianity. Nor was not pretty. It was often terribly violent and tragic.

When the Church and state unified, when flag and faith married, it became a nightmare than lasted a thousand years. Google the fall of Constantinople and then the Crusades and then the religious wars in Europe. Suffering for faith in Christ did not end when national churches were formed. It only changed form and Christians began killing each other. This is the truth that Christian Fascists want to hide. Suffering simply evolved from the murder of Muslims and the heathen to the murder of Christians who were not in the national church. The history of the church is not on balance good, it is a disgrace, it is a history of unbelievable sins, and the people whom the church killed more than any other were those within its walls.

Jesus also predicted this in one of the Gospels. He wrote in Mark 13: 9- 10:

'You must be on your guard. You will be handed over to the local councils and flogged in the synagogues. Because of me, you will stand before governors and kings as witnesses to them.'

Jesus said in John 15: 20-21:

'Remember what I told you: 'A servant is not greater than his master.' If they persecuted me, they will persecute you also. If they obeyed my teaching, they will obey yours also. They will treat you this way because of my name, for they do not know the one who sent me.'

Jesus also said in Matthew 5: 11-12:

'Blessed are you when people insult you, persecute you and

falsely say all kinds of evil against you because of me. Rejoice and be glad, because great is your reward in heaven, for, in the same way, they persecuted the prophets who were before you.'

No, Paul did not have a death wish. He simply wanted to be like Christ and identify with him. This included persecution and I don't think Paul had a problem with that. If that was the cost of following Jesus, then he was happy to bear it. A Christianity without the cross is not Christianity. It is like the church today. Indeed, the cowards who run the churches in the West are always too busy trying to secure as many tax exemptions as they can to avoid persecution. They are convinced that a faithful witness can come through special privileges in the state, and license to abuse, and yet at the same time throw themselves against both history and biblical witness. Maybe they have heard of the words of Jesus, or maybe they hope you have not. In Luke 9: 23-26, Jesus said these words:

'Then he said to them all: 'Whoever wants to be my disciple must deny themselves and take up their cross daily and follow me. For whoever wants to save their life will lose it, but whoever loses their life for me will save it. What good is it for someone to gain the whole world, and yet lose or forfeit their very self? Whoever is ashamed of me and my words, the Son of Man will be ashamed of them when he comes in his glory and in the glory of the Father and of the holy angels.'

Head in the clouds or seated in heaven?

Jesus does not expect, desire, or anticipate that his disciples would forge an alliance, maintain allegiance, or align themselves with anyone other than himself. He is their Lord, their Master, their King. For many Western Christians, this contradicts the Christian Fascism they celebrate and submit to, and thus, there is a profound and unresolved contradiction at the heart of their faith.

For many, the layers of racism, xenophobia, class culture, sexism, phobias, and ageism must be stripped away before one even sees a sliver of a Christian faith, and this is the problem. For many Christians, their faith is like make-up, it is put on in the morning and taken off at night. The genuine Christian however, is persecuted if he or she follows Jesus. The fake Christians rarely are because they are aligned with the national culture, politics, or religion. Persecution is inevitable, said Jesus, and yet, most Western Christians run to hide with the laws of the state and special privileges, arguing that friendship with the world is possible, desirable, and manageable.

Yet, in this alliance, compromises are made so that the *'Christianity'* that emerges is no longer with Christ as Lord. Christians who try to assert the Lordship of Christ are derided as fanatics, extremists, and fundamentalists, people with their heads in the clouds. Yet, the Bible demands that we choose: have our head in the clouds or be seated in heaven. In other words, is the belief in heaven, the return of Christ, and the eternal world having your *'head in the clouds'* or is it having certainty that our seats are already in heaven as Paul claims in Ephesians: *'And God raised us up with Christ and seated us with him in the heavenly realms in Christ Jesus' (Ephesians 2: 6).*

We have been considering Christian politics, properly said, to be the way Christians live in this world. This is important because, to live without fear, or without unhelpful fear, the Christian must have a foundation, and not be blown about by every wind of doctrine. Christian Fascism celebrates Christian nationalism, the good old days, the Christian heritage, traditional values, Christian values, and so on. None of them are Christian and these hypocrites do more damage to the Gospel and to the cause of God than anyone in the West. For them, it is about instilling fear in others, punishing others, and forcing them to comply with religious laws.

It would be better for the Gospel if the West had no Christian heritage or no Christian traditions as they so terribly hinder, frustrate, and undermine Christianity. Christian Fascism is concerned with promoting the politics of fear and division. These fascists are often aligned with their counterparts in the political and economic elites who have no interest in Biblical Christianity. There are no hearts harder than those of a religious bigot or hypocrite. Nothing can budge them. The churches in the West are full of them. This unholy alliance between Christian Fascists and secularists pivots Christianity in all the wrong directions.

Christians have their own politics with Christ as their Lord and

King. Jesus doesn't believe in democracy since he is the King. He doesn't align himself with our Culture War but expects our allegiance to him as it is his world. His name is above all names even the names that are on our lips constantly. He has at least one advantage over everyone you place your trust. God is eternal and the ones you worship will die. They are simply human, and they will perish. No matter how important their words, actions, thoughts, or policies are, they eventually run out of days and die.

There are three aspects to detoxifying manufactured political fear stoked by Christian Fascism. They are part of the Christian's new identity through their union with Christ by faith. They are opposed to everything that the Christian Fascist holds dear, and it is the reason why most churches will not touch any of these themes. If they do, they only address them in passing, and they will never address them directly. The Bible blows their political theology out of the water and sinks it as certainly and as decisively as the Nemesis sank the Chinese fleet in the first Opium War. Nemesis decimated the Chinese Fleet. The Word of God decimates Christian Fascism. One cannon volley from the scriptures will destroy anything the fraudulent filth of Christian Fascism will conjure with their master the Devil; in whose service they are dutifully employed.

We have already looked at two of them: the Biblical idea of the nations, what many call the Gentiles, and the nation of Israel. The nations have no destiny, no special purpose, and no hidden plan in God's plan. They are the pool from which the many people who will come to faith in Christ are drawn. There is no biblical mandate to save a nation, convert a nation, or bring a nation to Christ. Those who want to 'save' the nation are always Christian Fascists. It always leads to the slaughterhouse and the end of Christian testimony to Jesus. Nations are free to bring glory to God. That is God's gift to them. The Christian is to follow Christ, to seek out and save the lost, the lost sheep, those who wander, those who seek the truth in all the dark places, and those who are burdened with fear.

The second is free speech. We have shown that there is no such thing as free speech in the West and thankfully so since laws on slander and libel and malicious gossip exist to punish Christians who want to destroy the reputations of people they don't like. God also exhorts us to be careful what we say as the tongue is a terrible evil and capable of much destruction. We can come into the presence of

God through faith in Christ and we can speak to God in confidence, freedom of speech, and boldness.

The third aspect of Christian politics is political identity and the citizenship of the Christian. It is not on earth with skin allegiance or paper ties, but eternity, with God, and our home, is heaven. This is heresy for the Church as their ties are on earth in their buildings and their monuments, their churches. No Christian is to live with their head in the cloud and indeed, they cannot afford to, since as Paul reminds us, persecution is inevitable for the one who follows Christ. For the Christian, there is an alternative kingdom to the kingdom of the nationalist fascist, and that is the kingdom of God. That is why so few Christians in Church ever speak of the kingdom of God. It undermines their lifestyle.

'My kingdom is not of this world' said our Lord Jesus Christ, and Paul exhorts us in Ephesians that we are through Christ made into one new humanity in the Savior who broke down the wall of enmity that separates Jews and non-Jews, in his body on the cross. There is also no Jew or Greek, or slave or free, or male or female, but all are one in Christ (Galatians 3: 28). So, we are to rejoice in the Lord Jesus Christ, reject the life that celebrates human efforts and achievements, embrace God's righteousness by faith, and accept the inevitability of suffering for sake of following Jesus. This is hardly the prep talk for avoiding fear, right?

Is not the Christian faith to be one of escaping fear? If you knew that the path ahead was good even though it would be difficult, would you still walk that path? Jesus told his disciples that before a house is built, the cost is determined to go see whether it is worth it. Many people who embark on the Christian life have not thought it through. I can say with absolute certainty that no baby sprinkled with water ever thought it through. Then the story became the tension between a nominal faith and a genuine one, between Christian Fascism and authentic Christian witness. Then the question is: are we to live with our heads in the clouds or seated in heaven?

Are we to accept the Christian faith as a kind of idealistic fantasy, *'head in the clouds,'* or accept the hard-nosed certainties of Paul that it is worth the danger because in the journey we can truly know ourselves and the God who walks with us? Certainly, many people think that the Christian is one of those people with inner peace. I have never really understood what that was, or is, from Christ's point of view.

Many atheists also believe that Christianity has the qualities they respect, and that fit into the norms of modern secular society. It would be sad if that were the case. I don't see any compatibility and truly hope that Christianity and any other system of thought remain a counterpoint to the sterile materialistic hedonism of the West. The atheists mean Christian Fascism. They love these guys. It is always interesting to see heads of state and political leaders line up to go to church on Sundays with the Fascists.

The path of the cross, the path of Jesus Christians follow is about inner peace in the sense that we receive God's peace through our Lord Jesus Christ. But it is also one of inner irritation or inner frustration, not only inner peace. Inner peace is about staying still, reaching that happy place, and finding one's balance. For Christians, it is the opposite. It is the conflict, the inner turmoil that drives the Christian forward. It is not the lack of faith, fear, or the challenge of life, but it is the pursuit of the knowledge of God. Paul tries to explain this strange and seemingly contradictory view in Philippians 3: 12-17:

'Not that I have already obtained all this, or have already arrived at my goal, but I press on to take hold of that for which Christ Jesus took hold of me. Brothers and sisters, I do not consider myself yet to have taken hold of it. But one thing I do: Forgetting what is behind and straining toward what is ahead, I press on toward the goal to win the prize for which God has called me heavenward in Christ Jesus. All of us, then, who are mature should take such a view of things. And if on some point you think differently, that too God will make clear to you. Only let us live up to what we have already attained. Join together in following my example, brothers and sisters, and just as you have us as a model, keep your eyes on those who live as we do.'

It is our faith in Christ, our trust in him, and our confidence in the work of Jesus on the cross that drives us forward. Faith in Christ does not lead us to settle down and be content with the accomplishment of God for bringing us from death to life. He gave us his Spirit and his Spirit searches the deep things of God. This

Spirit works in our hearts his purpose which is to drive us to a deeper knowledge of God. It makes sense that the working out of this knowledge of Christ does not occur in church on Sunday or in the monastery cut off from the world but in life, in ordinary life.

I press on says Paul, and he moves forward. He does not go back. Behind is the past, yesterday and it is done. He continually moves forward, he strains to go forward, he lunges forward, and he presses onwards. All the language Paul uses has the idea of a destination and craving to reach that destination. What is that destination? Is it a nice church where you can meet your friends every Sunday and talk about your week? Is it that Bible Study where you drink nice coffee and gossip about people and open your Bible briefly and close it and then go back to your lives? No, the destination for Paul and our destination is heaven. He seeks heaven because he has membership there. Paul does not seek heaven to get to heaven. He will get there. Paul has a seat reserved for him. Christ is waiting for him. Christians need to rediscover eternity and rediscover heaven and realize that what we have here is not all there is, our home is heaven with Christ in God, our destination is to be with Christ, and we will all get there if we believe, but we need to keep moving forward.

The Christian Fascist (following their Master, Satan), keeps pulling us back to the past, to the traditions, to the heritage, to the nice building, and to the political power. We are to say no to these fascists, and we are to throw off everything that entangles and the sin that so easily deceives and look unto Jesus the author and finisher of our faith who for the joy that was set before him endured the cross, despising the shame, and sat down at the right hand of the throne of God (Hebrews 12:2). Like Christ, your membership, your citizenship is in heaven. You do not have your head in the clouds, but you are seated with Christ in God. It is the Christian Fascist who is in trouble, eternal trouble. They have their head in the sand and their eyes closed to God and their hearts hardened to the Spirit.

5   CITIZENSHIP

Our citizenship is in heaven

Only God knows the future. As the end of 2022 approaches, the world came very close to nuclear conflict over the civil war in Ukraine. There were a few weeks when this threat heightened, and the warmongers across the world put the lives of billions on the altar of political expediency. Nuclear war may yet be the legacy of America since it is the only nation that has used atomic bombs on civilian populations, though the French and British as well as the Russians and Chinese among others have tested countless weapons. Many of these nations, the ones who possess such terrible weapons claim to be Christian nations, but it is impossible to reconcile such policies with the identity and work of Jesus Christ.

A true Christian is a person who follows Jesus. Their identity is in Christ. Their citizenship is in heaven. Christian citizenship is not a spiritual allegory or metaphor in the New Testament. Heavenly citizenship is a reality, it is political citizenship. This is true politics. It is not surprising therefore that so many nations as well as the church have sought to kill Christians. We are not citizens of any nation but of heaven. Paul writes in Philippians 3: 18-21:

'For, as I have often told you before and now tell you again even with tears, many live as enemies of the cross of Christ. Their destiny

is destruction, their god is their stomach, and their glory is in their shame. Their mind is set on earthly things. But our citizenship is in heaven. And we eagerly await a Savior from there, the Lord Jesus Christ, who, by the power that enables him to bring everything under his control, will transform our lowly bodies so that they will be like his glorious body.'

Our citizenship is in heaven. The original Greek word is very interesting. To my knowledge, it is the only time this word is used in this sense in the New Testament. It is a word that was used outside the Bible texts to describe politics. Whenever it has been, it is not talking about some metaphorical sense of politics or allegiance but real political identity. This is a political term, not a religious term. Paul is not talking about dual citizenship here, a compromise where God wants us to balance our national citizenship with our heavenly one. It is not a *'practical citizenship,'* versus a *'citizenship in waiting.'* This is an exclusive political identity. It has nothing to do with the nation of America or the founding fathers or the Constitution, but it has to do with Christ.

This word *'citizenship'* in the Greek text means *'of the state or nation.'* That word in Greek for citizenship would have been well known in the world of Paul. Paul's readers would have known the nature of his assertion and its implications. It was radical, deeply subversive, and rebellious. It was *politeuma*, which mean a state or a nation, a form of government. Wait, what are you saying? Are you saying that the Christian, when he or she comes to faith, gains a new citizenship, one that is political, and the answer is clearly yes! Faith in Christ ushers you into new political citizenship, not tied to your church, your denomination, your nation, your ethnic group, or your family. It is in Christ.

For Christians, their old national identity, their passport is the past, and we cannot take it with us, it is nice to have to go from place to place, but our allegiance is not to their flag or to their wars or to their values, but to God. Our true loyalty is to God and him alone and to him alone do we submit in obedience. This is radical stuff. This is subversive. This is Christianity. Our old citizenship is convenient, and we can use it (Paul did) but our true citizenship is in heaven, with Christ. This is the good news. It is why Paul in Corinthians calls himself and his fellow evangelists, *'ambassadors for Christ.'* He writes, *'We are therefore Christ's ambassadors, as though God were making his appeal through us. We implore you on Christ's behalf, be reconciled to God' (2 Corinthians 5: 20).* Like the school children whose uniform testifies to their school and the school's reputation, Christians represent Christ to all they meet, they bear his uniform which is woven in grace and peace, and priceless as it was bought with a price, the blood of Christ shed for sin, where Jesus died for us, on our behalf so we might speak of him. The Christian is not interested in boasting in themselves, but rather *'to proclaim the virtues of him who called you out of darkness into his marvelous light' (1 Peter 2: 10).* The Christian tells of the virtues, the goodness, the morality, not of themselves, but of Jesus, the one who called us out of darkness into light.

This political way of thinking is also found elsewhere in the letter. In Philippians 1:27, Paul tells his readers:

'Whatever happens, conduct yourselves in a manner worthy of the gospel of Christ. Then, whether I come and see you or only hear about you in my absence, I will know that you stand firm in the one Spirit, striving together as one for the faith of the gospel.'

The phrase *'conduct yourselves'* is sometimes translated as *'your way of life'* but the meaning is lost in English, and this is probably because the translators want to hide the subversive nature of the letter. The word in Greek for conduct yourselves is *politeuesthe.* Yes, it is related to citizenship. Its proper meaning is to live as a citizen. We are to live as a citizen on earth, following Christ, our King. Jesus is King, not Caesar. It is interesting that both words, to conduct yourselves and the word for citizenship have the root of politics. They are political words. Simply by being a Christian, one is engaged in the politics of heaven, and one is free to be a Christian anywhere wherever one feels called to serve, in whichever nation one finds oneself.

This means that Christian Fascism has no Biblical foundation. Christian Nationalism is an offshoot of Christian Fascism and involves the efforts of people to mix flag with faith. Not only will it fail, but it does not meet with God's approval. To be truly free as a Christian is to walk with God, to follow Christ, and to do so *'whatever happens.'* It is about us, it always was, it was never about others, and this is what the Fascists get wrong. Faith is about my relationship with the living God, it is not about telling others how to live according to the laws of God. Paul says, *'conduct yourselves in a manner worthy of the Gospel of Christ.'* How can you tell others to follow God if you do not do so yourself? Even if you do, the message of the Christian is singular, it is *'be reconciled to God.'* There is no other message from heaven.

Christian Fascists will dismiss this argument. They have a different goal: killing people. Fascists always do. The Christian church murdered people for centuries. Christian Fascists today long for control of the state so they can start killing people again. They long to return to the nightmare of their religious pogroms and holocausts. Christian Fascists follow a different Master, perhaps you know his name. It is Satan. He is the ruler of this world, and politics is his domain. If Christian Fascists were even vaguely interested in freedom, they would talk about Christ, but they are more interested in forcing people to change.

For the Christian, we await the Savior the Lord Jesus Christ. This means that this world is not all there is, and this means that we are not to focus on the earth but focus on our relationship with God. This does not mean ignoring our obligations and duties but rather reshaping them and remolding them against our new citizenship and allegiance with Christ. A relationship with God enlivens and strengthens everything in our life, it should not detract from our life, but it should invigorate it and cultivate it and strengthen it. But we await the return of the Savior from heaven.

It seems to me that this is the problem for many Christians, they simply do not believe in heaven or that Christ will return. God exists to help them in their life now and they want the best, they want his promises even if they do not exist, and when they don't get them, they become resentful. They don't keep an eye on eternity and have both eyes on earth, they don't keep their ear to the scripture and the voice of God, but they have their ear twitching to the latest fad and fashion, they don't keep in step with God but explore all the alleys and backstreets of the world searching for anything but God.

Sometimes God is silent. Sometimes there is no answer from God, and we walk in the darkness. Sometimes there is no help coming. This is the life of a Christian. Remember Paul says, *'whatever happens.'* Following Christ is not just for Sunday, but for every day, it is not just for the good days but the bad ones. Those days will come. Being a follower of Jesus is not easy, that is why the church is so popular, you get it all out the way one hour a week and go back to normal, but that is not Christianity. The Christian will encounter his or her greatest challenge not in the world, but amongst others who call themselves Christians. Paul writes:

'For, as I have often told you before and now tell you again even with tears, many live as enemies of the cross of Christ. Their destiny is destruction, their god is their stomach, and their glory is in their shame. Their mind is set on earthly things. But our citizenship is in heaven.'

Paul graciously makes the meaning of this text clear: the essential problem with the enemies of the cross of Christ is that their mind is set on earthly things, their mind is set on the earth and not on heaven. We are not to get distracted by the phrase in the text *'their god is their stomach.'* This is a summary of their problem, but he is not taking aim at fat people or large people, but rather a way of life. The stomach is the heart of the person, the center of their being. For many Christians, their god is themselves, their gratification, their needs, and their wants. But it is worse because their glory is in their shame. Paul is also not referring to any form of immorality. No, they were probably upstanding and moral people, as most Christian Fascists are. The heart of their religion was not Jesus Christ, but themselves. Jesus and the cross meant nothing to them. They saw Jesus on the cross and turned away preferring to find solace in themselves and the world around them.

They were in fact living the life many Christians live today. The cross is the footnote, their salvation is self-effort, and they don't believe in eternity. For them, the cross is of no importance to their Christian life. For Paul it was everything and for the life of all true Christians, it is everything, for all who have their citizenship in heaven. Paul wrote in Galatians 6:14:

'May I never boast except in the cross of our Lord Jesus Christ, through which the world has been crucified to me, and I to the world'

Am I welcome?

One of the greatest fears in the world is the fear of being left out. It is the fear of exclusion. It is the fear of being unwelcome. This fear produces anxiety, a desire to retreat, leave and never return. This happens to most of us at some point in our life. I can think of many examples. I am sure you can too. If you want to feel the fear of exclusion, the fear of being unwelcome, and the fear of being left out, go to church and you will feel it. Churches are among the most unwelcoming places in the world. This doesn't bode well for a person exploring Christianity.

I have been told so many times by Christian Fascists that it is the responsibility of the visitor to make themselves feel welcome. It is the fault of the visitor if they feel unwelcome. Churches with lots of money (tax-free of course) employ a *'welcome pastor'* and their job is to welcome newcomers into the church. They are being paid to be nice to you. They have a format and a program and once that is over, you have been *'welcomed'* and they need never speak to you again. Ah, Western Christianity, it is a wonder anyone comes to faith. The answer is easy: few do, and one of the reasons is that there is more warmth in the Artic circle than in most churches.

If you meet someone and they say they have never felt unwelcome in a church, then I am sorry, but they are part of the problem and are spiritually blind. I would also surmise they are one of those lovers of the church, one of those converts the Pharisees traveled over sea and land to find. I am sorry, if they see only light in the church today, then their heart is in darkness and there is no hope for them.

Most people of all temperaments have felt the pangs I have described when they enter any kind of venue or event or place. They are perfectly natural feelings. Fear of the unknown is perfectly natural. You don't know anyone, you don't know the mood of the room or the atmosphere, and you don't know how people will respond. It takes confidence to enter a room or a place or a temple, (I mean a church, for that is what it is) and few can do it with ease. The rest do it with bravado. They keep their anxiety deep in their heart, away from public view.

The New Testament describes several encounters between the

apostles and people interested in knowing more about Jesus Christ or Messiah. These encounters are both instructive and informative. They tell us about the world of the first century, notably the divisions of the time, but they also tell us about the deeper spiritual implications of the message of the gospel or the good news concerning the Messiah. We will look at several examples of people who feared exclusion, feared being left out in the cold, and feared being cast aside, but who found acceptance, warmth, and love in Jesus.

These encounters are usually ignored by Christian Fascists over the centuries, especially between AD 500 and the last 50 years or so. You will find out why. These Fascists have clear ideas on who is excluded in their kingdom on earth. In the Bible, however, by contrast, everyone is welcome in the kingdom of God. No one is excluded, no one is left out, no one is better or worse than the other, and before God, all stand equal. This is of course the opposite message of the Christian Nationalists or Christian Fascists as I call them, who run the churches today.

Christianity is not the church and never has been. A Christian is a person who has a personal relationship with Jesus Christ and God the Father whom he sent, in the power of the Holy Spirit. To be a Christian is simply to know God. A Christian wants to know God more. There is a holy determination for personal spiritual growth, dare I say holy selfishness, a desire to grow and mature, and for others, the hand of friendship is always available and the heart of love not a spirit of judgementalism.

The Bible clearly teaches that all are welcome to know the Messiah, trust in him, receive him, and follow him, and all are equally welcome. There is no need for any to fear, no need for any to feel anxious about exclusion, no need to feel left outside in the cold. Jesus stands with his arms outstretched and says to you and to me:

'Welcome my friend, my brother, and my sister, my child, whom I love and for whom I came into this world. I have died for you. Come and see my wounds in my hands and my feet, they were for you. My life was lived out for you. I died for you so that you might live.'

We know this because of the Bible, where God's plan for our lives is revealed. Why then did the priests keep the Bible closed for

1,000 years, hidden in Latin, obscured by the blasphemy of the Mass? Why did the racist white preachers and sectarian bigots in the Western church promote segregation, slavery, and racial prejudice, and still do today? They kept the Bible closed. They didn't want the ordinary person to read the Bible for if they did, ordinary people would know that people in power were lying about God, the world, and about each other. If the Bible was open, then more people might have heard the good news of Jesus the Messiah, who came to bring life, hope, and peace to all who trusted in him.

I know what some of you might be thinking. It is all right for you to say this, and it is all right for you to claim to say these things, but am I really included? Am I welcome if I believe in this Jesus Christ, can I enter through the front door, or do I need to come in the back door and sit in the seats furthest from the front? Surely the front seats are reserved for the good people, the rich people, or the white people. Am I truly welcome? If he knew my heart and could see within, he would not welcome me. He would cast me out.

Friend, if Jesus will not welcome you, then who will? Jesus welcomes all who turn to him in faith, he welcomes all who want friendship with God, and he welcomes all who trust in him as the one who died for their sin and is their Lord and Master. Jesus welcomes all. It is in Christ we are welcome; it is in him we are accepted without reservation, and it is in him we are equal before God.

This is the message of Paul the apostle who wrote many of the letters in the New Testament. Christian Fascists hate Paul and the reason they do is he believed in the equality of all people before God, the radical idea that all people, regardless of their position or their past, their color or their creed, their culture, or their craft, all were equal in Christ and in the sight of God. He wrote in Galatians 3: 28:

'There is neither Jew nor Greek, neither slave nor free, nor is there male and female, for you are all one in Christ Jesus.'

Does this apply to me?

Does this apply to me? What you will find in life is that equality is a rare quality, indeed it is endangered and likely to go extinct. In Australia for example, most government programs are based on the principle of discrimination. People who save money are penalized and those who spend everything are rewarded with special benefits. Even many people who do not engage in tax fraud to cover their assets and wealth are excluded from a vast array of government benefits, while the people who do engage in tax fraud are welcomed by the state with open arms.

Democracy is effectively a reward system for the party faithful. After an election, the followers of the winning party are rewarded financially and those whose party did not win are excluded financially. The national funds are then distributed to the vested interests over the tenure of the party's reign with impunity. We call it 'pork barrelling' but it is in fact, corruption. It means equality is repudiated in favor of vested interests. This is not the way to run a nation, but for those who do not understand democracy, it is a simple explanation. The question that any loser to an election must ask is: does this apply to me? The answer will be, no, it doesn't. You get nothing.

The question: does it apply to me is also a question many ask when it comes to the Bible. There are two aspects here. The first is no and the second is yes. Let me explain. We must take care when reading the Bible, especially the Hebrew Bible, and the Old Testament. It has proved perilous for many who do not read it carefully. The context is always important. We need to read the text and see to whom God is speaking, who is the recipient of God's promises, the nature of these promises, and the position of these conversations in the light of the whole course of God's revelation.

Some people open the Bible at some obscure passage and find a phrase like *'And God said to go up'* and then think that this means that we are to go up and find a mountain and then live up there and buy a house and raise a family and spread the gospel to the people on that mountain. All these important life decisions were based on reading a phrase in the Bible that said, *'And God said to go up.'* In this context, God said something different. He told Israel to go up and fight their enemies in battle. That verse says nothing about the choices we need to make in life. It is an example of taking the Bible out of context, which is what we should strive to avoid.

When we read the Hebrew Bible, especially the narrative books, they are the history books, we need to ask the question: does this apply to me? If not, then that is fine. There are at least five other questions we can ask of any passage: 1) what is going on in this passage? 2) what does this passage tell me about who God is and what he is like? 3) what does this passage tell me about myself and what I am like? 4) what is the context of this passage, in the chapter or the Book? 5) how does the text tell me how I might know God, or understand him better?

These were the questions going through the mind of a man who long ago asked about a passage he was reading from the Hebrew Bible, the Old Testament. He asked the question that many of us ask today when we read the Bible: does this apply to me? It was a good question. This is the right question to ask. He was reading the Bible sensibly and we can thank God for it. It is recorded in Acts 8: 26-40. In it, the apostle Philip meets *'an Ethiopian eunuch, an important official in charge of all the treasury of the Kandake (which means "queen of the Ethiopians"). This man had gone to Jerusalem to worship, and on his way, home was sitting in his chariot reading the Book of Isaiah the prophet' (Acts 8: 27-8).*

The first thing that alerts me is that Philip does not meet a white man, he is not an American, or an Anglo-Saxon, and he does not speak English. Philip meets an African, an Ethiopian, a man whose skin color has excluded him from many Christian Churches for centuries, his skin color and ethnic identity had him segregated and cast out, but not for Philip and not for God. This man was reading the Hebrew Bible and was most likely a convert to Judaism as he had come from Jerusalem. While my white ancestors were running around in blue paint naked, confused, and illiterate, around the time of the Roman invasion of Britain, the Ethiopian culture was highly civilized, cultured, and elegant.

What does this mean? It means that white Christian Fascism is false. It is a fraud. The celebration of the Anglo-Saxon culture as the pinnacle of civilization is historically inaccurate. The Bible the fascists pretend to believe in, exposes their fraud. It always has. Philip met an African man reading the Hebrew scriptures. Does this apply to me, he asks, and Philip pays no attention to his skin color. It is not even remarked upon. The legacy of white supremacy is that for a thousand years, skin color meant exclusion and separation. In many churches and seminaries, skin color still does.

For God, it doesn't. All are welcome in the kingdom of God, even white people, even Americans. The apostles were color blind, and arguably most were in those days long ago. Multiethnic societies are not a recent creation. Racism is the West's great infamous legacy. I read recently that one famous Christian evangelist (George Whitfield) was a great defender of slavery and a slave owner. I didn't know. I was astounded. The books I had on his background had hitherto whitewashed that part of his biography. This means that his message of salvation was only for white people. That is not the Gospel, and it is not the teaching of Christ, nor is it found in the scriptures. All are welcome. Those Christians who look down on people of color are not Christians, they never were, and never will be. Many will struggle with forms of racism and prejudice throughout their lives, but a person who rejects people because of their ethnic background or their nation of origin, or their language, needs to seriously investigate the authenticity of their faith.

The second thing that alerts me is his sexual identity. He wasn't married with three kids living in a nuclear family. He was a member of a sexual minority. He was a eunuch. This means that he was officially castrated for his office in the palace as was common in those days across the world in ancient times. Being in this position was one of exclusion. In the Jewish faith, he was excluded, by virtue of his status from the full benefits of membership in God's people. Deuteronomy 23: 1 states that no eunuch may enter the temple of Jerusalem. Nevertheless, this prohibition did not deter him from the Hebrew Bible, nor did it dissuade him from seeking truth from a Bible that seemed to exclude him.

The fact that he looked to understand God in a faith that could not accept him fully showed an unusual degree of earnestness. He truly looked for understanding. But he was not without hope, and this was probably not his problem. Let me explain. The Hebrew Bible had several promises about a time in the future when eunuchs would be welcome as full members of God's people. I can assume that this man, had he read the scriptures would have been familiar with these promises.

For example, in Isaiah 56: 1, the very scroll he was reading on his chariot, the prophet says, *'my salvation is close at hand and my righteousness will soon be revealed.'* He went on to say, *'Let no foreigner who is bound to the Lord say, "The Lord will surely exclude me from his people." And let no eunuch complain, "I am only a dry tree"' (56: 3).*

The LORD, which is Yahweh, the Ancient of Days says through Isaiah these amazing words of promise (56: 4-7):

'For this is what the LORD says: "To the eunuchs who keep my Sabbaths, who choose what pleases me and hold fast to my covenant— to them I will give within my temple and its walls, a memorial and a name better than children; I will give them an everlasting name that will endure forever. And foreigners who bind themselves to the Lord to minister to him, to love the name of the Lord, and to be his servants, all who keep the Sabbath without desecrating it and who hold fast to my covenant— these I will bring to my holy mountain and give them joy in my house of prayer. Their burnt offerings and sacrifices will be accepted on my altar. For my house will be called a house of prayer for all nations."'

There was, therefore, an understanding for this man that Yahweh's promise was for full inclusion in the people of God. He looked forward to it, not just looking for the Messiah, as did the Jews, but for the excitement of being fully embraced by God.

In the Acts episode, Philip and the eunuch talked about Isaiah (Acts 8: 30-36):

'"Do you understand what you are reading?" Philip asked.

"How can I," he said, "unless someone explains it to me?" So, he invited Philip to come up and sit with him. This is the passage of Scripture the eunuch was reading:

"He was led like a sheep to the slaughter, and as a lamb before its shearer is silent, so, he did not open his mouth. In his humiliation he was deprived of justice. Who can speak of his descendants? For his life was taken from the earth."

The eunuch asked Philip, "Tell me, please, who is the prophet talking about, himself or someone else?" Then Philip began with that very passage of Scripture and told him the good news about Jesus. As they travelled along the road, they came to some water and the eunuch said, "Look, here is water. What can stand in the way of my being baptized?"'

The third thing that leaps out at me is the natural way Philip and the man talk about the good news of Jesus and his simple baptism in the river. Philip meets the man where he is. He is reading the Bible and he does not understand it. Philip explains that Isaiah is not speaking of himself but of the Messiah, Jesus. He was the lamb of God, led to the slaughter, sacrificed for the sin of the world. His death was one of injustice and humiliation, but in that death, he achieved the purpose of God, which was to become sin, to become the scapegoat for our sin, so that all who trust in him might have eternal life. The text simply reads: *'Then Philip began with that very passage of Scripture and told him the good news about Jesus.'* He started with Isaiah and moved on to other parts of the Hebrew Bible that spoke of the Messiah. Philip does not talk about the church, or a building, or a tradition, but *'about Jesus.'* This is the good news. The good news is about Jesus. It is not about me, it is not about my church, it is not about America, or democracy, or freedom, or Donald Trump or the Left or the Right, but it is about Jesus.

The most remarkable and moving part of this encounter is his immediate desire to be baptized and in this, we see the Ethiopian finding some water and Philip baptizing him there. Curiously, it is not public and there is no one to see it, which suggests it does not really matter. Jesus said if two or three are together, I am in your midst (Matthew 18: 20). This is a blessing.

So, does the salvation of God apply to all? Yes, it does, even to a white man, even an American. The ancient promises of the prophets told of a time when salvation would be open to all who believe, and that all would be included, welcomed, and accepted, without reservation. The good news is not good news about the church, or a building, or a denomination or creed, but *'about Jesus.'* It is all about Jesus, who he is, what he has done, and our relationship with him. Does it apply to me? Yes, it does, to all of us, without reservation.

Will you accept me?

Will you accept me? It is an awful thing to realize you are not welcome. It might hit you when you open the door, and there is that cold silence, those frosty looks, the looks of contempt, and the eyes that avert their gaze. Or maybe, everyone is polite, and you get the impression that you are welcome, but slowly you realize they are just saying what needs to be said, going through the motion, as we might say in Australia, or mouthing the required words and phrases, but in their heart, they are just waiting for you to leave. I prefer the authenticity of hatred to the falseness of fake piety any day.

It has been my experience over the years that most churches are generally disinterested in new people. They have their cliques and their groups, and they really don't want to get to know new people who might disturb their social circles, many of which have been carefully cultivated over the years, trimmed, and cut like a hedge, and the last thing they need is something new. Most churches will be polite but not friendly and they will not welcome you. It is only at the end of their decline that these bigots will notice the generation gap, and as they fondle the dentures, they grumble to each other and will say *'we need more young people in this church,'* but by then it is too late.

Churches tend to oppose newcomers and new ideas. The identity of most is not in Christ, but in their ethnicity by birth or their political affiliation. *'Sit down, shut up, and do as you are told'* is a central doctrine in many places. After several centuries of appalling racism, the Western Church still has not grasped the central message of the gospel – all are one in Christ (Galatians 3:28). Not only in America or Australia, but many national churches define God in terms of their own ethnic filters and yet he is the God for all. All are welcome, and all are equal before God. It is such a simple message and yet how difficult it is for so-called Christians to follow and adopt.

When I returned to Australia, I was deeply shocked at the racism amongst Christians, even at the seminary. I had experienced racism in the Japanese church as well, but when I returned, I naively thought that the old Australian white supremacy had died out, but it had not. It never left. My parents raised me with genuine Christian values of treating everyone the same and of avoiding prejudice. What I realized later was that my parents were in the minority, even in the church. I simply assumed that all Christians adopted Galatians 3:28, but I have since realized that most Western Christians ignore it. God doesn't.

Peter, the apostle, struggled with favoritism. His struggle was a microcosm of the early Christians in Jerusalem, the so-called

'Followers of the Way,' Jews who had come to faith in the Messiah, who had set up shop in the temple courts and met for prayer and reading the scriptures. There is no sign they celebrated the Mass or practiced infant baptism. They were men of prayer, hospitality, and service to the poor. Many of these men held to the view that Jesus had come only for them and that for anyone to have faith in Christ, they needed to become a Jew, follow the Law of Moses, and adopt all the customs and traditions. All new converts could believe in Jesus the Messiah, but they needed to be circumcised, follow the food regulations, live like a Jew, and tack Jesus on top of centuries of religious rituals.

The relationship of the Law of Moses with the freedom of the Spirit was the chief tension in those days, between self-effort and grace, between religion and faith. Paul speaks about this sect in his letters (Romans 2: 25-29, 1 Corinthians 7: 19; Galatians 2: 12, 5: 6-13; Ephesians 2: 11; Philippians 3: 3, Colossians 2: 11; Titus 1: 10). Both the letter to the Hebrews and James presents a scathing critique of this circumcision sect.

If the leader of the Italian regiment Cornelius in Caesarea had not appeared on the scene it is quite possible that Peter might have apostatized and joined this Jewish countermovement against the Followers of the Way. It was a turning point in the history of early Christianity. Cornelius was a convert to Judaism, probably like the Ethiopian eunuch. He was a centurion, therefore a Roman soldier, and he was according to Acts 10: 2 a man who had deep reverence and respect for God as well as authenticating his faith by caring for the poor. He received a vision from God to send men to Joppa and bring back Peter who was living by the sea (Acts 10:1-7).

From our perspective, it seems a remarkable thing to happen, but we are about to discover something secret, something horrible, something bizarre that has been lost to history for some reason. It was even lost to Peter and to the early Jewish Christians. This is despite the commission of Jesus to preach the good news to all nations (Matthew 28: 16-20), despite the day of Pentecost and the arrival of the Spirit, and the proclamation of the message of the gospel in all languages in the ancient world (Acts 2). Peter had forgotten the words of Jesus: *'For God so loved the world that he gave his only Son so that whosoever believes in him shall not perish but have everlasting life' (John 3: 16).* To our shame, many

Christians forget too. God loved the world, not just me, not just America, not just white people, not just our tribe, but all tribes.

Is Jesus your God or is he for everyone?

One of the most hideous things about being in the Church of England is the idea that God is for the English, that God is English, that God speaks English, and that Jesus is an Englishman. It sounds completely stupid, but in practice, it is the common belief of many people in England and around the world. The liturgy of the Anglican Church, a poor imitation and copy of the Roman Mass and the Prayer Book, a plagiarized version of the Missal, (written before copyright laws), is drenched in English culture, English values, and the Satanic English class system.

The Anglican Church is a relic of Imperialist Britain, a celebration of the Empire, genocide, and colonialism. At full steam, if one has the misfortune of attending High Mass at one of the so-called High Church services, with robes, incense, and choral music, one feels that one is no longer in Sydney or Nairobi or California in 2022, but one has been transported to the days of British India with half-naked locals holds large fans for the women in long dresses and men in army tunics, before the Indian Mutiny.

Anglicanism is out of date, it belongs in a museum, and many of its leaders can go there too to be stuffed like birds or extinct animals. The Church of England is a lesson in history and the misappropriation of faith, the corruption of the glorious gospel of Christ, and how godless a nation can become when it only pretends to follow God. The Church of England, or the Anglican (English) church as they like to be known these days is the breeding ground for Protestant Christian Fascism.

Peter also had a similar view to the Anglicans, one that was out of date. He and many early Christians had a broader belief in an exclusive faith. They believed that only Jews could find salvation in the Messiah Jesus. They honestly believed that non-Jews, from the nations, could have no real or equal part in the Savior Jesus the Messiah or the Christ. He says so in Acts 10: 28:

'He said to them: *"You are well aware that it is against our law for a Jew to associate with or visit a foreigner.'* In most translations it reads 'Gentiles' but this is a polite rendering. The Greek word means foreigner or one of a different nation or race. Peter believed this. He believed in the Law of Moses and up to this encounter with God he had no problem reconciling this xenophobia with his belief in Jesus as his Messiah. This was spiritual xenophobia, but before we judge him, this has also been the attitude of most Western Christians for centuries. Their attitude to foreigners or poorer people, people of a different class, or people of a different background or religious affiliation have fallen foul of their own prejudice as they deny the good news of Jesus to anyone and everyone who is not in their group.

I have always struggled with Peter's lack of faith in this, his spiritual xenophobia, and his reluctance to see the global extent of the love of God found in the Lord Jesus Christ. I am deeply thankful to my mother and my uncle as well; for the way they showed Jesus Christ to me and did not hesitate to embody and live out Galatians 3: 28 in their daily lives. I do not judge Peter, because *'but for the grace of God go I,'* but the Hebrew Bible is full of passages that predict or foreshadow a broader enfranchisement of the covenant than the nation of Israel. *'Come let us go up to the mountain of the LORD,'* says Isaiah (2: 3). There are the stories of Rahab, Ruth, Naaman the Syrian, and the widow of Zarephath to name a few. The Hebrew Bible, whilst clearly anointing Israel, is equally clear on the broader extension or coverage of the salvation of the LORD. How could they not see it? How could they be so blind to this anticipation? They certainly allowed prostyles, and this reflected, in part, their appreciation of this future enfranchisement of the promises of God.

I believe that this is a forgivable misunderstanding as the first generation of people who came to faith in Christ. I do not blame them, nor do I judge them. I do not however forgive the people of the nations who have come after them and have chosen to divide the kingdom of God down ethnic and nationalistic lines. What Christian Fascists have done and continue to do is the blaspheming of God's name among the nations and the quenching of the Spirit. The only divide that makes any sense in the Bible is between the Jewish people and the nations, and the apostles explain how the good news of Jesus is for all people, regardless of their national origin. The racism, bigotry, and national Christian Fascism that the West embraces, make absolutely no sense from a Christian perspective, nor from even the most liberal interpretation of the New Testament.

You see, Peter needed a vision from God to convince him that the Law of Moses no longer applied and that foreigners could come to faith in Christ as equal partners, on equal terms, as siblings in Christ. There were several aspects to this. First, he received the worst possible vision from God, one that was deeply offensive and challenged his assumptions. In his vision, he saw a tablecloth of food, with all the creepy crawlies that he was forbidden to eat under the Law of Moses (recorded in Acts 10: 11-16).

'He saw heaven opened and something like a large sheet being let down to earth by its four corners. It held all kinds of four-footed animals, as well as reptiles and birds. Then a voice told him, "Get up, Peter. Kill and eat." "Surely not, Lord!" Peter replied. "I have never eaten anything impure or unclean." The voice spoke to him a second time, "Do not call anything impure that God has made clean." This happened three times, and at once the sheet was taken back to heaven.'

Now, it is interesting what happens next. Peter begins to think about the vision and how it applied to food and then his mind goes beyond food to other things such as people. God did not say, *'welcome foreigners Peter,'* but he said, *'kill and eat.'* God left it up to Peter to work it out for himself.

God does that with us. He gives us his word and tells us his truth and often, he leaves it up to us to work it out. His Spirit does the work in our hearts. Do not think that anything is too hard for God. He was able to work in the life of Peter, so nothing is too difficult for him.

Peter travels to see Cornelius with other Jewish Christians and when he arrives, he realizes he is in the presence of lots of foreigners. He must have guessed at this, but he tells them plainly the reality of the state of Israel at that time, the relative position of Jews and Greeks, even foreigners who had come to faith in the God of Israel, like Cornelius. He tells them that he is not allowed to associate with foreigners or visit them, but that God had shown him a vision and yes, he had worked it out:

'But God has shown me that I should not call anyone impure or unclean' (Acts 10: 28).

Peter said nothing about food. He had worked it out. The Spirit had told him to go and see the Roman (Acts 10: 19-20). It is about 63 km (about 39.15 miles) these days to go between the two cities and so along the road, Peter pondered and worked it out. God doesn't rush us. He helps us work things out in our own minds. When Peter arrived, it all becomes clear.

Peter tells them that he realizes that God shows no favoritism and that he calls both Jews and foreigners to have a relationship with Jesus Christ, the Messiah. Peter preached to them about Jesus, a summary of the life and person of Jesus, and our need to trust in him. Once again, the focus is Jesus. Luke writes in Acts 10: 44-47:

'While Peter was still speaking these words, the Holy Spirit came on all who heard the message. The circumcised believers who had come with Peter were astonished that the gift of the Holy Spirit had been poured out even on foreigners. For they heard them speaking in other languages and praising God. Then Peter said, "Surely no one can stand in the way of their being baptized with water. They have received the Holy Spirit just as we have."'

This episode is the neglected day of Pentecost when the Spirit fell on foreigners as well as Jews. Why it is neglected by the Church is not a mystery because the Church tried to remove the Jewish origins of the faith such as dissecting the beauty of the Passover into the monstrosity of the Mass. Fortunately, the text of the scriptures has remained intact. Perhaps it is because the church expects few to bother reading it beyond the sectarian bigotry of their nationalist church. Peter, not Paul is the great transformation of a Jewish man. He is the one, along with Philip, who took the Gospel to the nations, to those who were not Jews. Philip seems to be the most relaxed of the three men and seems to glide in and out of history with ease. Paul needs to be knocked off his horse and blinded, while Peter is shown the offensive vision and God allows him to work it out for himself.

For Peter, God has no favorites. The only real division was between Jews and non-Jews and Peter tells us there is no difference.

So, why has the church made so many divisions, and why do people think Christianity is an American religion or an English religion? Why is China shutting down churches out of fear that they are spreading American values? Christianity is not American. When you feel the fear of rejection at church, or amongst people who call themselves Christians by whatever barrier they impose know this: God has no favorites. God treats everyone the same. There is one Savior for all, Jesus the Messiah, who calls all to believe and follow him.

What is the good news about Jesus?

When I first moved abroad, I lived in Japan, in a city to the north of that great nation, called Sendai, where I lived for a few years. I am happy to call that place my Japanese hometown. I threw myself into the culture, history, and language of that society, making the most of each day, visiting temples and shrines, festivals, and events, and exploring historical ruins including castles. It was a rich cultural experience; one I will never forget. It changed my life and my views on the world as well as shaped my own faith in the Lord Jesus Christ.

At the end of my time there, a Japanese person said, '*you know more about Sendai than the people in Sendai.*' It was a funny remark. I am sure the people of Sendai knew more about their city than I did, but what he was suggesting, and applauding was my willingness to deepen my understanding of Japan as much as was humanly possible. After 3 years, I discovered much about the great nation of Japan, its language, history, culture, and traditions.

For Christians, it is the good news about the Lord Jesus Christ that is the heart of their faith. It is the reason they are Christians. Yet, for many, who claim to be Christians or think they are, the phrase '*good news about Jesus*' is poorly understood, ignored, downplayed, or marginalized in a faith that is more about them and their lives. The good news for the Christian is not about the effects of faith, but the source of faith, the object of faith, and the reasons for faith which have to do with another. It is good news because it is good news from God, not from us. It is good news because it is good news about God, not about us. It is good news because it is good news for us, not good news because of us.

Just as I threw myself into my life in Sendai, anyone who comes to faith in the Lord Jesus Christ, that is genuine faith is never content with a superficial understanding of Jesus. A true Christian is not interested in the Christian view on politics or the Culture Wars or Christian Fascism or morality, but they are interested in Christ, they want to know more about Christ, and they want to ponder, review, and celebrate the good news about Christ. What do you think of Christ is the question all people must answer, for upon the answer to this question lies their eternal position before God. What we think of the Lord, who he is, what he has done, and why he is good news, is the question all Christians ask themselves for he is truly their life.

It is highly likely that Cornelius, the centurion of the Italian Regiment in Caesarea in Israel, had heard of the man Jesus of Nazareth. News traveled fast in those days, and the ancient world seemed to have postal and monetary systems, well-kept roads, and regional safety that makes our crazy, messy, dangerous world rather primitive. Peter didn't say, *'well guys, you know about Jesus, there is nothing new to add here.'* That would be the church's response and they would add, *'please add your donation at the door, we need money for the church roof or the pastor's new house, and if you genuinely love God, you will cough up the dough.'*

No, Peter's focus began and remained on Jesus Christ. That is how you know the good news. If the minister, pastor, or priest goes off to another topic such as morality, the Culture Wars, or something else and Jesus is but a footnote, then leave that church and never go back. Christianity begins and ends with the Lord Jesus Christ and the good news concerning him. What does Peter say? It is recorded in Acts 10: 34-43:

'Then Peter began to speak: "I now realize how true it is that God does not show favoritism but accepts from every nation the one who fears him and does what is right. You know the message God sent to the people of Israel, announcing the good news of peace through Jesus Christ, who is Lord of all. You know what has happened throughout the province of Judea, beginning in Galilee after the baptism that John preached— how God anointed Jesus of Nazareth with the Holy Spirit and power, and how he went around doing good and healing all who were under the power of the devil because God was with him.

"We are witnesses of everything he did in the country of the Jews and in Jerusalem. They killed him by hanging him on a cross, but God raised him from the dead on the third day and caused him to be seen. He was not seen by all the people, but by witnesses whom God had already chosen—by us who ate and drank with him after he rose from the dead. He commanded us to preach to the people and to testify that he is the one whom God appointed as judge of the living and the dead. All the prophets testify about him that everyone who believes in him receives forgiveness of sins through his name."'

There are five things I would like to draw your attention to. First, there is something Peter knows, or rather has discovered. God does not show favoritism. He treats both Jews and non-Jews in the same way and his principle is simple: those who do what is right and revere and respect God from all nations are those whom he accepts. In effect, what he is saying is that God accepts those who seek him, those who look for him. Cornelius revered God and considering this, he helped the poor, he did not oppress them. Those who seek God are those who most likely want to turn to him and believe in him.

Second, there is something Cornelius knew or something he had discovered. There was a message in the town in the city that had gone forth across the nation about Jesus of Nazareth, who had the Holy Spirit, who after being baptized by John, *'went around doing good and healing all who were under the power of the Devil because God was with him' (10: 37-8).* This is the message most have concerning Jesus: Jesus the healer, Jesus the miracle worker, the brother to all. This was not, however, the full message.

Third, the good news about Jesus was that peace would come to all through him because Jesus was Lord of all. Verse 36 says: *'You know the message God sent to the people of Israel, announcing the good news of peace through Jesus Christ, who is Lord of all.'*

This is the difference between Jesus the miracle worker and good man and Jesus the Messiah. Peter's claim is that *'you know'* this message, this information. You know that Jesus came to bring peace because he is the Christ, the Messiah, the expected anointed one of God and this Jesus is Lord of all. He is not just Lord of the Jews, but of the Romans, the Greeks, the Americans, the Asians, and the Africans. He is the Lord of all. He shows no favoritism.

The fourth thing is something that Peter had known before the vision and that was his experience with Jesus was real. He saw him, he knew him, he lived with him. Peter says in verses 39-40: *'They killed him by hanging him on a cross, but God raised him from the dead on the third day and caused him to be seen.'*

This is the eyewitness account of Jesus who lived died and rose again. To waver on this is to cease to have any Christian faith. There are many who claim that all that matters is some nebulous, ethereal idea of *'love'* but they are wrong. The Christian faith is based on historical assumptions about what happened to Jesus: his death, burial, and resurrection. He rose, he was seen, and he was real. Christianity is a faith based on historical events. Many Christian Fascists will scoff at this and say that all that matters is some moral principles and allegory for life, and so on. Why do you pay these charlatans money? Leave their churches and never return. They are fake churches, and they are fake Christians. Jesus died and Jesus rose again. That is Christianity.

The final thing that leaps out at me is the message that Peter was commanded to speak and it was this message that Cornelius had not heard. It was the message that he needed to hear. It is the message we all need to hear, for it is good news but it is hard news to hear, for it is not easy news to listen to, and it is difficult news to accept. Luke wrote in verses 42-43: *'He commanded us to preach to the people and to testify that he is the one whom God appointed as judge of the living and the dead. All the prophets testify about him that everyone who believes in him receives forgiveness of sins through his name.'*

What this means is that what you think of Jesus has eternal significance. It is significant because Jesus has been appointed as the judge. God the Father will not judge, but Christ will. Judgment is in his hands. But judgment is not according to what we do, or our works or the charitable deeds of our life, but what we think of Christ: *'...everyone who believes in him receives forgiveness of sins through his name.'*

No one is excluded from the good news about Jesus. Everyone is included. Everyone needs to make a personal decision about Jesus. Everyone needs to make up their mind. All are equal before God. There are no special groups in the kingdom of God, there are no 'front row seats' there is no special pass for corporates or the rich. Americans, Russians, Chinese, and everyone else are on the same level. All who believe in him, trust in him and accept him receive forgiveness of sins. This forgiveness is full, complete, and eternal, and with God, there are no favorites. All are invited, and no one is turned away. This is the good news.

Why does God welcome me?

There is no fine print in the Christian faith. There is no hidden agenda, no secret knowledge, no deeper code to unravel, no catch, no tricks or cunning plan. I can give no guarantee for a church you may attend. I don't know. I have long said since I began Freedom Matters Today, that Christianity and the Church are not the same. Churches often have their codes, their languages, their rules, their rituals, and their circles, but not Jesus Christ, not the Bible, and not Christianity. There is no fine print tucked away.

The Bible is usually straightforward and clear, most of it. There are sections that might confuse such as the allegories of the Revelation of John or the sensual subtleties of the Song of Songs. Overall, the writers of the Bible, especially the New Testament wrote to people, hence they are letters or circular texts for a variety of localized communities. They wrote to be understood.

The Gospel writers and Paul, among others, wrote to convince their readers that Jesus was the Christ, the Messiah, the one promised to the people of Israel and in whom all might find hope, peace, freedom, and life eternal, through knowing him by faith. The goal of Paul is to show that all are welcome in Christ. Why does God welcome me? That is why Jesus came into the world, to welcome all to eternal life.

Now, one of the fears many people have about faith is that God will not welcome them, that he might welcome others, but that he will not welcome them. There are many reasons put forward as to why many people feel this way. They do not doubt the message of the good news concerning Jesus Christ, they hope it to be true, they hope that they might be welcome, and they hope that the promises of God might apply to them.

This hope is based on the fear that somehow, somewhere, sometime, God will withdraw his favor, his love, and his promise to them. Often their reasons are based on what the church has taught them, or life has taught them, or what their own heart has taught them, but at the end of the day, their fear is baseless, it is a fiction of their own creation, and the sooner they replace that fear with the assurances of God's word the better.

Paul tells us in Galatians 3:28 a similar thing to what Peter told the Roman Centurion: God has no favorites. This should be a source of great assurance to everyone for what it means is that there is no fast track to faith, no special path for the chosen, and no lucky breaks for the rich. All must pass the same way; all must face the same problem, and all must embrace the same Savior.

The way of all people is to recognize their need for God, to see the salvation of God, which is Jesus Christ, and to understand the way of salvation, which was his terrible death on the cross. The way to God is not through me but through the cross, not my broken body, but his, not my broken heart, but his, not my broken relationships, but his. He stood in my place where I could not, in my stead, on my behalf and he welcomed me. Paul wrote: *'There is neither Jew nor Greek, neither slave nor free, nor is there male and female, for you are all one in Christ Jesus.'*

What Paul is saying here is that all people who are Christians have one thing in common, one thing that makes them who they are, one thing that bridges all their differences, and this has nothing to do with them. It has nothing to do with their race, their background, or their gender. It has to do with their status in relation one to another. They are all *'one in Christ Jesus.'* Paul's primary concern in Galatians is to show that faith in Christ is simple but life-transforming, it is a personal decision to trust, and not based on deeds or actions, and that it links both Jews and Greeks together. It is this personal faith in Christ that brings about our restored relationship with God. Faith is a significant theme in Galatians. For example:

'a person is not justified by the works of the law, but by faith in Jesus Christ' (2: 16).

'I have been crucified with Christ and I no longer live, but Christ lives in me. The life I now live in the body, I live by faith in the Son of God, who loved me and gave himself for me' (2: 20).

'Scripture foresaw that God would justify the nations by faith and announced the gospel in advance to Abraham: "All nations will be blessed through you"' (3: 8).

'...no one who relies on the law is justified before God, because "the righteous will live by faith" (3: 11).

'But Scripture has locked up everything under the control of sin, so that what was promised, being given through faith in Jesus Christ, might be given to those who believe' (3: 22).

'So, in Christ Jesus, you are all children of God through faith' (3: 26).

'For in Christ Jesus, neither circumcision nor uncircumcision has any value. The only thing that counts is faith expressing itself through love' (5: 6).

Therefore, Paul is saying to the Galatians, and he is saying to us today that what divides us is of no importance to God, it does not cloud his vision, his decision, or his perception of us. Those who have faith are 'in Christ' and are all *'one.'*

There is therefore no reason to fear exclusion because it is Christ who brings us together as one, not ourselves. If we believe, there is no room for fear, no room for anxiety, we can stand with the rich and powerful, with the Greek or the Jew, with men or women because our standing before God is not in ourselves but due to another, it is due to Jesus Christ. All are one in him, and without him, none can stand before God.

6   BEYOND CHRISTIAN FASCISM

Revisiting Faith and Flag

In this book, we have been challenged to think about the relationship between faith and flag by opening the Bible and seeing what God has to say about it. It is the mixing of faith and flag that is at the heart of Christian Fascism, one of the offshoots being this new far-right movement called *'Christian Nationalism.'* All Christian Nationalists are fascists, but not all Christian Fascists are Christian Nationalists. A Christian Fascist is a person who has confused the message of the gospel, the good news about Jesus Christ with their nation. They mix flag and faith, and they end up twisting the gospel of Jesus Christ, turning it into a slogan for nationalist, moral rejuvenation. Fascism began in the church and has been around for over a thousand years. If you would like to read more, please consider my book: *Freedom from Fascism, A Christian Response to Mass Formation Psychosis,* where I explore this subject in more detail.

Jesus came to make disciples of all nations, not save nations, not make Christian nations. Nowhere does Christ or any of the apostles advocate Christian Fascism. The apostles have a singular purpose, to proclaim the identity and the work of Jesus and what this means for us and our relationship with the Father. There is never an agenda for moral rejuvenation outside the transforming work of the Holy Spirit in sanctifying us and setting us apart by the blood of Christ shed for us on the cross. The good news of Jesus is open to all people, without conditions, qualifications, and tests. It is free to all.

In the past, fascists twisted the gospel by adding something to it, such as baptism, a temperance pledge, or more recently, marriage or gender affirmations. This latest twist, the insistence that Christians must agree that marriage is between men and women, or affirmation of the two genders, is completely unbiblical. History will record this sexual obsession of the Western church as just another failed fascist movement to kill the good news of Christ. God will not tolerate his gospel sharing pride of place with the latest fascist proclamation of who is in and who is out. If these fascists want to obey God, let them pay taxes, after all, that is what the God they pretend to believe in calls them to do (Romans 13: 6-7).

Most major Christian sects together have their origins in the West and reflect the ethnic and cultural values of that nation of origin. Sadly, most of the sects used violence to oppress their own people who believed that God wanted them to worship in a different way, gather in a different way, or read the Bible in a different way. The Pilgrim Fathers left England to start again in America because they were being persecuted and killed by the fascists who ran the Church of England. For centuries, the churches murdered each other, started wars, hoarded wealth, and destroyed nations, and finally after they could not kill anymore, alternate sources of wealth arose to challenge, overthrow them, and create the modern societies we have today. Even though we live in a capitalist-style society, the old, corrupt, church aristocracy survived, with its putrid values, its abiding Anti-Semitism, and its corruption. Today, Christian Fascists ache for a return to money and power, and the sword.

The greatest threat to faith in the world is not the state but the church and especially the church that mixes flag and faith. We are seeing a revival of this evil today in America, Australia, and Europe. Christians become fascists when they give up on Christ. Churches that promote moral rejuvenation are always promoting something the Bible was silent about. I cannot find any verses in the entire Bible to support their political agenda. The fascists counter and say, *'America is a Christian nation,'* which is a surprise to the millions who are not Christians. But which Christianity are these fascists talking about? These Christian churches all hate each other, that is perhaps all they have in common. The best they can come up with is this nebulous, vacuous, meaningless term called *'Christian Nationalism,'* which echoes marginalized white supremacy. This is not the gospel. It never was, and never will be.

Is America God's Enemy?

In this book, we have looked at the question: *'Is God on America's side?'* and the answer is unequivocally *'no.'* The Bible is silent on the matter of nations, and while he is not on America's side, he is also not against America. God's main concern is the elevation of his Son, the Lord Jesus Christ, and what people think of him, and how they might respond to him, whether to reject him or follow him. Christianity is about Jesus, not America. Jesus came to save all people, even Americans, even those who administer empire and power, for there is a greater power than Washington and that is the grace and mercy of God found in the forgiveness of God through the death of Christ on the cross.

There will always be an America, there will always be someone, somewhere who wants to rule the world, there will always be the abuse of power and the corruption of the highest political office. If, as a Christian, you want to make America a Christian nation, you will fail. Many have tried and failed. We all need to stand before God and give an account of our lives, how we spent them, and what we did with them. God does not promise what he does not promise, and he did not promise a Christian America, nor did he promise a perfect society, nor did he say that democracy and Christianity are synonymous. God never approved the US Constitution, and the sooner American Christians appreciate the beauty but frailty of this human-inspired centuries-old document the better. The best this world will be is a complete mess.

When Jesus spoke to Pilate, he said *'my kingdom is not of this world.'* This was the Son of God, who could have taken the world by force, but he did not. He was a man of peace, a man of love, and a man of grace. He died for the sin of the world so that all who place their faith and trust in him have eternal life. I certainly will not say that he wants us to reform society, or force change, or kick people out of political office, or bring about a revolution. The only revolution that matters is that of the human heart when God steps in and turns a man or a woman from death to life, from despair to hope, and from sadness to joy. Only God can do that, and all the great powers of America, cannot change one person's heart. What America leaves the world is up to them, history will make its choice.

The Christian is not called to foment revolution, or to effect political change, but to follow Christ. It is as simple as that. We walk by the grace of God found in the reality that God stood in our place, on the cross, to take our sins upon himself, so that the punishment, the guilt, the shame, the power, and the evil of sin might fall on him, and not on us. This is our motivation, our spiritual urge, if you will, to keep in step with the Spirit who has been given to us.

Our citizenship is in heaven, true freedom of speech comes through speaking to God, and Jesus calls us to make disciples of all nations. This is the political identity of the one who follows Christ. The simple message of the Christian is not telling people what to do but pointing them to the identity and work of Jesus. We are, as Paul reminds, us 'Christ's ambassadors,' and we have one message for the people of all nations:

'Be reconciled to God. God made him who had no sin to be sin for us so that in him we might become the righteousness of God' (2 Corinthians 5: 20-21).

Remember, freedom matters today, because you matter to God.

ABOUT THE AUTHOR

Michael J. Sutton is the founder and CEO of Freedom Matters Today, which looks at freedom from a Christian perspective. He holds a Ph.D. from the University of Sydney (2002), a Master of Divinity from the Australian College of Theology (2017), a Diploma of Bible and Ministry from Moore Theological College (2017), and a First-Class Honours Degree in Economics (Social Sciences), from the University of Sydney, 1995. He spent ten years of his working life in Japan as a lecturer and researcher in international relations and economics in Sendai, Tokyo, and Kyoto. He lives in Sydney. His first book, *Freedom from Fascism, A Christian Response to Mass Formation Psychosis,* was published by Hidden Road Publishing in November 2022 and is available through Amazon.

WHAT IS FREEDOM MATTERS TODAY?

Freedom, Matters Today is a tax-paying, educational service provider that looks at freedom from a Christian perspective. We are apolitical and non-sectarian. To date, we have identified six themes: freedom from fascism and tyranny, freedom from fear and despair, freedom from past and prejudice, freedom from guilt and shame, freedom from sin and death, and freedom from war and conflict.

Our slogan is: *'don't go to church, follow Jesus instead.'* Being a Christian is not about going to a building on Sunday but about having a relationship with God. Religion leads to the church, but faith leads to God. God gives us true freedom.

Our books are works of originality and rely upon the arguments and perspectives of the author. They avoid name-dropping or name-calling. There are few, if any, footnotes. If you require verification, Google it. This book is based on our blog and podcast written and broadcast between May 9 and June 4, 2022.

New Testament Greek exegesis reflects the author's academic training but also draws from Strong's Concordance, and BDAG, or *A Greek English Lexicon of the New Testament and other Early Christian Literature*, Third Edition, edited by Frederick William Danker, University of Chicago Press, 2000.

For further information about Freedom Matters Today, listen to our podcast, broadcast weekly, or visit our website at freedommatterstoday.com. We explore faith, life, and what it means to follow Jesus

Remember, Freedom Matters Today, because you matter to God

www.ingramcontent.com/pod-product-compliance
Lightning Source LLC
Chambersburg PA
CBHW071001040426
42443CB00007B/614